As the policemen pushed and kicked King along the sidewalk toward the county jail, his followers and admirers, both black and white, gathered and watched in alarm.

Then the alarm turned to anger. Some began shouting threats of retaliation as they chased after King and the policemen. King simply turned toward the crowd and raised a hand and shook his head. It was a gesture some had seen before, and they knew what it meant. Nothing good could come from repaying violence with violence.

"The beauty of nonviolence," King would later write, "is that it seeks to break the chain reaction of evil."

A Background Note about
MARTIN LUTHER KING, JR.

Life's persistent and urgent question is, "What are you doing for others?"   —Dr. Martin Luther King, Jr.

From the time he was a young boy, Martin Luther King, Jr.'s greatest desire was to help others. He grew up in an era when African Americans were often denied basic rights that many people take for granted—such as the right to vote, the right to eat dinner at a nice restaurant, and even the right to choose a seat on a bus.

King first experienced racism as a very young child, when his best friend, who was white, told him that they could no longer play together. His friend's father did not approve of his son having a black friend. The idea that skin color could be used as a reason to destroy the bonds of friendship was astonishing and heartbreaking to the young Martin Luther King, Jr. It was, perhaps, at that very moment that the seeds of desire to help his own race were planted in King's heart.

However, the cost of selflessness was high. During the years that he devoted nearly all his time and energy to the cause of civil rights, King was repeatedly yelled at, spit on, threatened, and thrown in jail. Once, his home was even bombed. Still, King never failed to believe two things: change for the better was always possible, and the only way to achieve that change was through peaceful protest, not through violence.

This is the story of the man who led a movement that changed not only the lives of many Americans, but also the hearts and minds of people around the world; a man who remembered his past and dreamed of the future when he said, "I have a dream that my four little children will one day live in a nation where they will not be judged by the color of their skin, but by the content of their character."

MARTIN LUTHER KING JR.

WARRIOR FOR *PEACE*

TANYA SAVORY

TP THE TOWNSEND LIBRARY

MARTIN LUTHER KING, JR.
Warrior for Peace

TP THE TOWNSEND LIBRARY

For more titles in the Townsend Library,
visit our website: **www.townsendpress.com**

Illustrations © 2010 by Hal Taylor

All new material in this edition is
copyright © 2010 by Townsend Press.
Printed in the United States of America

0 9 8 7 6 5 4 3 2

Townsend Press, Inc.
439 Kelley Drive
West Berlin, NJ 08091
permissions@townsendpress.com

ISBN-13: 978-1-59194-202-3
ISBN-10: 1-59194-202-0

Library of Congress Control Number:
2009943313

Contents

CHAPTER 1

In the summer of 1928, in a small crossroads town in southern Georgia, a young black man named Joshua stopped for gas. He was on his way to visit friends in Florida during his vacation, and it had been a long drive from his home in New York. He stepped out of his car to stretch as he waited for an attendant to come out and pump the gas. Sitting on the porch of the rundown store near the gas pump was a young white woman, who watched Joshua with narrowed eyes and a scowl.

When Joshua saw the white woman staring at him, he took off his hat and nodded at her with a friendly smile. Immediately, the woman got up and walked into the store, slamming the door loudly behind her. Joshua was puzzled. He'd heard all the stories about how difficult life was for black people in parts of the South, but surely there was nothing wrong with being polite. Seconds later, two white men walked slowly out of the store. One was carrying a baseball bat.

"You a long way from home, ain't you, boy?" one of the men said after glancing at Joshua's license plate. The men continued walking at a steady pace toward Joshua, both of them wearing cruel grins.

"I . . . I just need to get some gas, sir," Joshua said, backing away nervously and reaching behind him for his car door.

"Don't serve niggers here," the other man barked. "Particularly niggers who flirt with our white women."

Without warning, the bat came down on the back window of Joshua's car, shattering it. As the man lifted the bat again to break another window, Joshua jumped into his car and started the engine in a panic. As he pressed his foot on the accelerator, he heard another window shatter.

Three months later, in Selma, Alabama, an elderly black woman approached the county courthouse with a look of determination. This was the third time she had tried to register to vote. Every time she had been to the registration office, there had been a new excuse. Most recently, the young woman behind the desk had told her that they were out of registration forms.

"When will you have forms?" the black woman had asked politely.

"No idea," the white woman had said, not looking up from filing her nails. "Could be a long, *long* time."

Now, a few weeks later, the black woman approached the desk again.

"I'd like to register to vote," she said patiently.

The young white woman barely glanced at her. "Sorry. We're closed for the day."

"But," the black woman began, pointing to the OPEN sign on the door, "that sign there says—"

"Don't care what the sign says," the woman behind the desk snapped. "If I say we're closed, we're closed. Now get on outta here."

Two months later on a cold winter morning in Montgomery, Alabama, a fifteen-year-old black girl boarded a city bus for the long ride across town to visit her sick grandmother. The bus was nearly full. There were no seats left in the "colored only" section in the back, and there were only a few near the front. The girl took one of the last seats, but just as she sat down, a white man boarded the bus.

"All right, girlie," the white bus driver called back to her. "You know the law. Move on to the back of the bus and stand there. Give the man your seat."

For just a moment, the girl sat still. *It doesn't seem fair*, she thought bitterly. *I'm no different from him except for the color of my skin*.

"I said *move!*" the bus driver yelled. "This bus ain't goin' anywhere until you get on back there with your kind."

The girl moved to the back and stood staring out the window as the bus began to roll along again. *Some day*, she thought angrily, *I am not going to move. I'm going to sit in that seat no matter what. Some day, things are gonna change*.

It was into this world that Martin Luther King, Jr., was born on January 15, 1929. It had been nearly sixty-five years since the Civil War and the end of slavery in the United States. Abraham Lincoln's Emancipation Proclamation had freed black people throughout the country, but, as many black people would discover, freedom did not guarantee equal or even fair treatment.

Particularly in the Southern states, where plantation owners had fought very hard against freeing the slaves, many black people found life to be nearly as miserable as it had been when slavery was legal. They were denied land, decent homes, and the right to have any kind of political power. Many white Southerners were especially nervous about former slaves becoming educated.

"Educate a nigger, and spoil a good field hand" became a popular saying in the South in the decades following the Civil War. Education equaled power, and many white people feared that blacks, who often outnumbered whites in parts of the South, would begin to gain an upper hand.

As a result, if a black man's crops were too successful, one morning he might find them destroyed. If his house was too nice, it might be burned down. And if he was too smart or demanded to be treated fairly, he could be beaten—or worse. Groups of white men known as "lynch mobs" roamed parts of the South, and sometimes the North, keeping black men, women, and even children in what they considered their rightful place: beneath white people. Too many times, black people were killed by these mobs. The sight of a black corpse hanging from a tree became a gruesome symbol of racism. It is estimated that between 1882 and 1927, 3,302 black people were killed by lynch mobs in the United States. Rarely were the murderers ever brought to justice.

When Martin Luther King, Jr., was growing up, many of these shocking practices were far too common. Even more common were "Jim Crow" laws. These were laws that enforced "separate but equal" facilities for black people. Many white people did not want to have to see black people in their stores, restaurants, movie theaters, hotels, schools, or even their public restrooms. Therefore, separate areas and facilities for black people were created that were supposed to be equal.

But they were *never* equal.

Until 1954, blacks would have to endure filthy, rundown conditions in public facilities labeled COLORED ONLY. They would be forced to sit in the back of buses and in back rooms of restaurants. Their schools would be rundown and underfunded. If they wanted to travel by train, they would have to board a separate car altogether— usually a car that was dirty, lacking seats, and at the very end of the train.

Back in 1892, when Jim Crow laws had been around for only a few years, a group of people, both black and white, in Louisiana had seen right away that the laws were unfair. Separating people based solely upon skin color seemed ridiculous. This group came up with a plan to prove how silly and wrong it was. One of the members, a young man named Homer Plessy, bought a first-class ticket to ride on a train in the "whites only" section.

As Plessy boarded the train, no one looked twice at him. He was just another white passenger taking a seat in his designated area. However, after Plessy sat down, he informed the conductor that he was one-eighth black. Immediately, the conductor told Plessy that he would have to move to the "colored only" car near the back. By Louisiana law, someone was considered black if they had any black heritage at all. Plessy refused to move and was arrested.

Homer Plessy and his group took their case to court, claiming that the separation of races was both confusing and unconstitutional. After all, according to the United States Constitution, all citizens, regardless of race, were to be treated equally. However, the judge, John Ferguson, didn't see it that way. Plessy and his group did not give up. They took their case all the way to the United States Supreme Court in 1896. Still, after much consideration, even the highest court in the land decided that separating races was not illegal as long as facilities and opportunities were equal.

Thus, one of the most famous decisions in American history came about through the *Plessy v. Ferguson* case. In 1896, it was declared that racial separation (known as "segregation") would be protected by federal law. "Separate but equal" became a way of life for many black people for the next sixty years. However, it took very little time for black people to become painfully aware that there was nothing equal about this law.

Despite all of the inequality that surrounded Martin Luther King, Jr., as a boy, his memories of childhood were mostly happy. Looking back on growing up, King would later write, "I had no basic problems or burdens. I was in a family where love was central and where lovely relationships were ever present."

King, or "M.L." as family and friends would call him all through his youth, grew up in a mostly-black neighborhood of Atlanta known as "Sweet Auburn." It was an area of working-class black (and some white) families; no one was rich, but there was very little poverty. The centers of the neighborhood were the churches, and M.L.'s father, who was often referred to as "Daddy King," was the minister of the popular

Ebenezer Baptist Church. Everyone knew and respected the King family, and even though M.L. had been born right at the beginning of the Great Depression, his father had a faithful congregation, so times were never hard.

M.L. was a typical kid in most respects. He played baseball and basketball with neighborhood friends, attended church every Sunday, showed off to girls, and got into a little trouble now and then. M.L.'s parents noticed early that M.L. was a very sensitive child. Once, when they passed a line of poor people waiting outside a soup kitchen, M.L. was moved nearly to tears to think that some people didn't have enough to eat. In the world he had experienced, everyone had what they needed, life was good, and everyone got along.

However, as M.L. became school-aged, several incidents made him painfully aware that people did not get along everywhere as well as they did in Sweet Auburn.

One of M.L.'s best friends was a white boy whose father owned a store across the street from the King home. When the boys started school, they were sent to separate elementary schools—one for whites and one for blacks. This did not surprise M.L., but what happened shortly after the school year began hurt him deeply.

One afternoon, the white boy met M.L. as he crossed the street to come over to play. Without any explanation, M.L.'s friend simply informed him that they were no longer allowed to play together. That night at the dinner table, M.L. asked his parents why on earth his best friend couldn't play with him anymore. Daddy King gently explained that it was because M.L. was black and his friend was white.

"For the first time, I was made aware of a race problem. I had never been conscious of it before," King would later write in his autobiography. "I was greatly shocked, and from that moment on I was determined to hate every white person."

Of course, as M.L. grew older, he would change his mind about hating white people, but King recalled that, at the time, he wondered, "How could I love a race of people who hated me and who had been responsible for breaking me up with one of my best childhood friends?"

It was Daddy King who reminded his angry son that he must love his enemies. And it was also Daddy King who showed his son that he should never allow others to treat him as though he was worth less because of his skin color. M.L. would always remember the time he and his father went shopping for shoes, and the white salesperson asked them to take a seat in the back of the store if they wanted service.

"There's nothing wrong with these seats. We're quite comfortable here," Daddy King had said calmly.

"Sorry, but you'll have to move," the white clerk had responded.

"We'll either buy shoes sitting here, or we won't buy shoes at all," M.L.'s father had said. At that point, he took his son's hand and walked out of the store. He looked down at M.L., shook his head, and said, "I don't care how long I have to live with this system, I will never accept it."

As for M.L.'s mother, she gently repeated to her son, during this difficult time of realization, that he was "as good as anyone." She explained that he would encounter Jim Crow laws, cruel people, and a system that would constantly make him think he was not as good as a white person. Still, he must not let it turn him bitter.

One of M.L.'s favorite things to do was to sit up front at his father's church and listen to the visiting ministers who came to preach from time to time. M.L. was amazed by the energy, the passion, and the connection with the congregation that these ministers displayed. Dozens of church members would raise their hands and shout out words of praise when the minister really got going.

One particular Sunday, M.L. listened to a minister speak in a way that he had never heard before. The man used words that sounded like poetry—long, complicated words that M.L. didn't understand. Still, M.L. listened closely. From his earliest years, he had been fascinated by language and by how just the right words could move people to tears or make them jump to their feet in excitement. Now, this minister spoke in a way that fascinated M.L.

That evening, M.L. talked to his father about how the words had made him feel. "You just wait and see," M.L. said confidently. "When I grow up, I'm going to get me some big words."

Not many years later, M.L. got his first opportunity to move people with words. As a fourteen-year-old, he entered a speech contest and won. His subject was "The Negro and the Constitution." The speech began:

> **We cannot have an enlightened democracy with one great group living in ignorance. . . . We cannot have a healthy nation with one-tenth of the people ill-nourished, sick, harboring germs of disease which recognize no color lines—obey no Jim Crow laws.**

The speech went on to point out that while the United States Constitution had amendments to protect the rights of black people, their rights were often denied.

The contest had taken place in a town fifty miles away from Atlanta, so M.L. had traveled there on a bus with a teacher accompanying him. Later that evening, the first-place trophy in his hands, M.L. was forced to move to the back of the bus so that white passengers could have his seat near the front. When M.L. hadn't moved quickly enough, the bus driver had yelled rudely at him. The irony of it all did not escape young Martin Luther King, Jr.

Years later, King would write: "I would end up having to go to the back of that bus with my body, but every time I got on a bus I left my mind up on the front seat. And I said to myself, 'One of these days, I'm going to put my body up where my mind is.'"

CHAPTER 2

By the time M.L. was nearing the end of high school, teachers and other adults began calling him by his name, Martin, instead of his childhood nickname. However, students at Booker T. Washington High had a new nickname for him: "Tweed." Martin was known as a stylish dresser, often wearing tweed suits to school, complete with cuff links and highly polished shoes. It wasn't just that he wanted to dress well—he quickly discovered that his suits, along with his elegant way of speaking and writing, attracted girls.

Though he was the son of a minister and was expected to act the part of a preacher's son, Martin preferred dancing and parties to church events. Martin was neither tall nor unusually good-looking, but his charm often made him the center of attention at parties. Daddy King disapproved of his son's behavior and punished him with both groundings and whippings. Martin's father was a stern and outspoken man who never failed to express exactly how he felt—particularly to his own children.

"This quality of frankness has often caused people to actually fear him," Martin would later recall. "I have had young and old alike say to me, 'I'm scared to death of your dad!'"

Martin was never "scared to death" of his father. In fact, he admired his father deeply, once writing, "I have rarely met a person more fearless and courageous than my father." However, Martin did learn to avoid arguing with his father and, whenever possible, he followed Daddy King's wishes. But as Martin approached college, he found himself in a difficult position.

One of Daddy King's greatest wishes and expectations was that Martin would also become a minister and would someday take over the preaching duties at Ebenezer Baptist Church. While Martin was growing up, his father often talked about the time when Ebenezer would be Martin's church. However, Martin had gradually lost his fascination with visiting ministers, fiery sermons, and rambunctious congregations. He began to think that all the shouting and excitement was undignified and failed to give proper respect to religion.

"I didn't understand it, and it embarrassed me," Martin would later explain. "I often say that if we, as a people, had as much religion in our hearts and souls as we have in our legs and feet, we could change the world."

Furthermore, Martin questioned faith and religion. He was taught that the Bible was an accurate historic record, as well as a guide for beliefs and morals. Even at a young age, however, Martin had once "shocked his Sunday school class by denying the bodily resurrection of Jesus." In fact, his primary reason for wanting to be baptized when he was a boy was that his older sister was getting baptized. Martin didn't want her to get ahead of him at anything—even salvation! And so, as Martin got closer to leaving for college, he began to consider studying either law or medicine, an idea he kept hidden from his father.

Martin's family assumed that he would attend Morehouse College in Atlanta. Morehouse was a well-respected college exclusively for black men. It had been established just two years after the end of the Civil War. Both Martin's father and grandfather had gone to Morehouse, and now it was Martin's turn. Because so many young men were off fighting in World War II in

1944, Morehouse offered high school juniors the opportunity to begin college a year early if they could pass an entrance exam. Martin passed the exam, and because he had skipped the eighth grade, he would begin college at the young age of fifteen.

The summer before starting college, Martin traveled to Connecticut for a seasonal job working on a tobacco farm. Connecticut seemed like a different world to Martin. He was amazed that he didn't have to use separate "colored only" drinking fountains and that in a fancy restaurant he could sit in the same room with white people. They didn't seem to be bothered at all by his presence. In a letter to Daddy King, he wrote: "On our way here we saw some things I had never anticipated to see. After we passed Washington there was no discrimination at all. The white people here are very nice. We go to any place we want to and sit anywhere we want to."

As Martin rode a train back home at the end of the summer, he was cruelly reminded of the life he was returning to. As he entered the dining car, he was led to a table behind a curtain so that the white travelers would not have to see him as they dined.

"I felt as if the curtain had been dropped on my selfhood," Martin would remember.

"The very idea of separation did something to my sense of dignity and self-respect."

Separation had also done something to Martin's education prior to arriving at Morehouse College. "I shall never forget the hardships that I had upon entering college," Martin later recalled. "Though I had been one of the top students in high school, I was still reading at only an eighth-grade level."

Martin's "separate but equal" high school had *not* been equal. The education he had received had been barely above average, and now he would have to work extremely hard to keep up with his college-level studies. Luckily, Martin enjoyed reading. Although he still attended his share of parties, he started becoming more serious about his future. Still, he didn't know exactly what he wanted his future to be. He had begun to settle on medicine until he discovered that he didn't really like all the science classes he would have to take. For nearly two years, Martin struggled to choose a major.

Although Martin's grades were only fair (mostly B's and C's) he attracted the attention of Morehouse College's president, Benjamin Mays. Mays had been the son of slaves, growing up in poor conditions in South Carolina, yet he worked hard and eventually received his Ph.D.

from the University of Chicago. Mays was also a minister, and he understood Martin's dislike of raucous congregations and overly emotional preachers. Mays often mentioned to Martin that many black ministers had not gone to college and received degrees in religion. They learned to preach simply by watching other ministers.

Many Sundays, when Martin listened to Dr. Mays preach, he was struck by how thoughtful, controlled, and intellectual Dr. Mays's sermons were. When Dr. Mays spoke about the problem of racism, he did not scream and shout and work the congregation into a frenzy. Instead, he talked about how black and white people must work together, and avoid anger and bitterness. In time, Martin's feelings about the ministry began to change as a result of Dr. Mays's example and friendship.

Martin's feelings about white people also began to change during his years at Morehouse. Although he had once been determined to "hate every white person," his work with a group called the Intercollegiate Council erased those feelings. The Council was made up of students from many universities, and one of the goals of the Council was to help achieve racial equality. Martin soon realized that many white students, even in the South, felt just as strongly as he did about Jim Crow laws and segregation.

Martin began to see that a minister could be someone who helped his congregation deal with the difficult times they lived in. Perhaps he could motivate black people to work peacefully for change. Martin would later look back and recall that he simply had "an inner urge to serve humanity." All he knew was that he wanted to help the black community. Near the end of his senior year, Martin made up his mind: he would become a minister after all.

After graduating from Morehouse when he was only eighteen years old, Martin went on to attend Crozer Theological Seminary in Pennsylvania in 1948. A seminary trains people to be priests, ministers, or rabbis, and Martin would spend the next few years learning how to be the kind of minister he dreamed of being. Martin was no longer the young man who couldn't say no to a party or a dance. In fact, as he later wrote, he went a bit overboard with seriousness, doing everything possible to avoid fitting the stereotype that some white people had of black people. Sometimes he even told other black students to dress better or to keep their dorm rooms cleaner—something that, at first, did not increase his popularity.

> **I was well aware of the typical white stereotype of the Negro, that he is always late, that he's loud and always laughing,**

that he's dirty and messy, and for a while I was terribly conscious of trying to avoid identification with it. . . . I'm afraid I was grimly serious for a time. I had a tendency to overdress, to keep my room spotless, my shoes perfectly shined, and my clothes immaculately pressed.

In time, Martin's seriousness about his appearance would loosen up, but his focus on his studies would remain strong. Once, his mother had written to him wondering why he never sent letters with news about the fun things he was doing and the people he was meeting in Pennsylvania. Martin wrote back, explaining, "I never go anywhere much but in these books."

Still, Martin traveled through a world of ideas and met many amazing people in the books he read. One particular man that Martin read about impressed him so much that Martin would follow his ideas for the rest of his life. That man was Mahatma Gandhi. Like Martin, Gandhi had experienced painful discrimination. Gandhi lived in India during a time when India was under British rule. Indians were treated in much the same way that many blacks in the American South were treated. They were forced into low-paying jobs, were given no political power, and were separated from the British so that the British could feel superior to them. Ultimately, Indians were made to feel worthless and unwanted in their own country. Many of them had become so frustrated and angry that they wanted to go to war with the British. They believed that fighting and killing was the only path to change.

However, Gandhi had a different idea. He urged Indians to protest by way of noncooperation, nonviolent marches, and peaceful resistance—not through fighting and bloodshed. In Gandhi's view, violence never solved anything, and it certainly never led to change for the better. "An eye for an eye makes the whole world blind," Gandhi often said.

When the British army tried, on many occasions, to break up marches or gatherings by using violence against the Indians, Gandhi begged his followers not to fight back. He instructed them, instead, to fall to the ground and pray. If the British continued to beat them with sticks, they should pray harder. Although Gandhi was a Hindu, he closely followed the teachings of Jesus Christ. "The gentle figure of Christ," Gandhi once said, "so patient, so kind, so loving, so full of forgiveness that he taught his followers not to retaliate when abused or struck, but to turn the other cheek—I thought it was a beautiful example of the perfect man."

Gandhi had strong faith in the goodness of human beings. He believed that the great majority of people on this earth hate injustice and are disgusted by the cruel treatment of weaker groups of people by those who are powerful. Gandhi sensed that, in time, the British in India who mistreated Indians would be shamed into stopping their bullying and discrimination.

He was right. However, it took years. Thousands of Indians were beaten and thrown into filthy prison cells, and hundreds of innocent Indians were killed. Gandhi himself was arrested numerous times and spent a total of nearly seven years in various prisons. When Indians fought back violently on a few occasions, Gandhi fasted until they returned to peaceful resistance. His followers did not want to see their leader starve himself to death, so they promised to turn the other cheek. Even if they were beaten bloody, they would not fight back with anything other than words and prayer.

Little by little, the world became aware of what was happening in India, and people were outraged. In particular, British citizens in England were horrified and embarrassed by their own government's behavior. Many British people began protesting their government's brutal treatment of Indians, and eventually the majority of Britons felt that the rule of India should be returned to Indians. In 1947, it was. Nonviolence had worked. It had changed the world.

Martin Luther King, Jr., was so amazed and inspired by what Gandhi had done that he bought every book he could find written by or about him. The same year that Martin entered Crozer and began his intense study of Gandhi's nonviolent movement, Gandhi was shot and killed by a man who had not agreed with his ideas. After Gandhi had worked continually for decades to bring about change through peaceful methods, his violent murder was a bitter irony.

Martin, along with the world, mourned Gandhi's death, but Martin's ongoing study of the man changed his life. It was during this time that a young Martin Luther King, Jr., began to wonder if the same kind of nonviolent methods could be used to lift black people in the South out of the discrimination they had endured for so long. Martin had always believed that the idea of "turning the other cheek" only worked between individuals, not between groups or nations. He had thought that when nations disagreed, war was the only answer.

"But after reading Gandhi, I saw how utterly mistaken I was," Martin would later write. "Christ furnished the spirit and the motivation, while Gandhi furnished the method."

In 1951, Martin Luther King, Jr., graduated at the very top of his class at Crozer. Daddy King wanted his son to return to Atlanta and begin taking over the assistant minister's role, but Martin was not quite ready to begin preaching yet. In fact, he was again beginning to wonder if he wanted to be a minister at all. He had been offered a scholarship to Boston University to study for his doctorate in theology, and he began thinking about teaching religion in a college or a seminary. He knew he would have to have a doctorate to do that, so he accepted the scholarship.

Martin was excited about moving to Boston. During the time of slavery, Boston had been a center of the antislavery movement, and it had never had Jim Crow laws. Remembering his days working the summer job in Connecticut, Martin looked forward to living in a city that did not discriminate against black people. However, Martin quickly learned that racism was not limited to the South. When searching for an apartment near the university, he could not figure out why every apartment had "just been rented" when he showed up to look at it. Soon, he realized that landlords who told him that the apartment was no longer available were using that as a phony excuse not to rent to a black man.

During his first year at Boston University, Martin avoided racial politics, even though he constantly thought about the troubles of his race. Martin was focused on preparing for his future. However, that future included something more than a graduate degree—it also included a wife.

"I had met quite a few girls in Boston," Martin would later recall, "but none that I was particularly fond of. I was about to get cynical."

Just when Martin thought he would never meet the right girl, he visited a friend from Atlanta who was studying music at the New England Conservatory of Music, also in Boston.

"Do you know any nice, attractive young ladies?" Martin asked without much hope in his voice. Martin's friend smiled and handed him the phone number of a young woman who was studying singing at the Conservatory.

Her name was Coretta Scott.

CHAPTER 3

"A mutual friend of ours told me about you and gave me your telephone number. . . . I'd like very much to meet you and talk to you," Martin said when he called Coretta later that evening.

Coretta Scott had already heard about Martin. Their mutual friend, Mary, had told her that Martin would be calling, and she gave Coretta a little background on Martin. Years later, Coretta recalled, "The moment that Mary told me the young man was a minister, I lost interest, for I began to think of the stereotypes of ministers I had known."

Even so, when Martin called, Coretta was polite. "Oh, yes, I've heard some very nice things about you," Coretta said, agreeing to meet Martin the next day for lunch.

"I'll come over and pick you up," Martin said smoothly. "I have a green Chevy that usually takes ten minutes to make the trip from Boston University, but tomorrow I'll do it in seven."

When Coretta first saw Martin, she was not impressed. He was shorter than she thought he'd be, and there was nothing particularly interesting about his appearance.

"He radiated charm. When he talked, he grew in stature," Coretta recalled. "I knew immediately that he was very special."

The two lingered over lunch, talking about many things—Coretta's music studies, world politics, Martin's dreams for the future. Finally, when it was nearly time to leave, Martin gazed at Coretta for a long minute.

"The four things I look for in a wife are character, intelligence, personality, and beauty," he finally said. "And you have them all. I want to see you again. When can I?"

Understandably, Coretta was stunned that Martin was mentioning marriage on a first date. She was flustered and simply responded that he could call her again, and she would check her schedule. Coretta was immediately drawn to Martin, however, in the same way that he was drawn to her. Still, she had worked hard to get into the New England Conservatory, having first studied voice at a college in Ohio and then being awarded a scholarship to study further.

Coretta was not sure that marriage was part of her plan just yet.

"She wanted to be a concert singer," Martin would later write of Coretta. "She was a mezzo-soprano and I'm sure she would have gone on into this area if a Baptist preacher hadn't interrupted her life."

As Martin and Coretta began dating regularly, Martin made it quite clear that the woman he married would need to set her career plans aside, raise children, and be at home waiting for him in the evenings. In her autobiography, Coretta would later explain that Martin Luther King, Jr., was in no way opposed to women having careers, and he totally supported women having the same careers as men. He just didn't want that for *his* wife.

Martin took Coretta home to Atlanta to meet his mother and Daddy King. He hoped desperately that his parents would like her, but he was worried. For years, Daddy King had insisted that Martin would return to Atlanta after all of his schooling, marry a girl from an important black family in Atlanta, and settle down as co-pastor of Ebenezer Baptist Church.

However, none of Daddy King's plans were Martin's plans now.

"Coretta, do you take my son seriously?" Daddy King asked Coretta sternly, not long after they had met. Coretta was confused by the question. Thinking that Daddy King was referring to a joke Martin had just told, she smiled and said no. At that, Daddy King looked relieved and proceeded to tell Coretta about the various young women in Atlanta that Martin had been seeing before he left for Boston. He suggested that Martin would probably marry one of these girls when he returned home.

Coretta looked at Martin, who sat across the room looking embarrassed and fidgeting with his hat. He never said a word that evening, knowing that his father would be angry about his intent to marry Coretta. But a few days later, Martin went to his father and quietly, but firmly, told him that Coretta was his choice. Nothing was going to change his mind.

Martin and Coretta were married on the lawn of Coretta's parents' home in Marion, Alabama, on June 18, 1953. Daddy King had softened in his attitude toward Martin marrying Coretta. In fact, he liked Coretta very much. He had happily agreed to be the minister at his son's wedding.

After the festivities were over, Coretta and Martin drove into the small town nearby to spend their wedding night—at a funeral parlor!

"I suppose it does sound funny," Coretta would recall, "but one has to realize there were no hotels with bridal suites for African Americans in that part of the country."

The undertaker was a friend of Coretta's family, a man who lived and worked in a big house near the center of town. The house had several guest rooms, so it was not the first time that black newlyweds in Marion, Alabama, had spent their first night in a funeral home.

After finishing his coursework at Boston University in 1954, Martin struggled to decide whether he should teach or preach. Finally, he settled on being a minister. He concluded it was the profession that would give him the greatest opportunity to help people. Then, when Martin was offered two pastoral positions—one in New York and one in Montgomery, Alabama, he had another decision to make. He and Coretta discussed it at length. How frustrating would it be to raise children where Jim Crow laws would hold them back and beat them down? How difficult would it be to return to the intense racism of the Deep South?

After many late-night talks, Martin and Coretta made up their minds. Martin wanted to serve. He wanted to reach out to black people and help them. He didn't want to choose the easier road and miss serving the people who might need him the most. He and Coretta would move to Montgomery.

"The South, after all, was our home," Martin explained. "Despite its shortcomings, we had a real desire to do something about the problems that we had felt so keenly as youngsters. . . . And we had the feeling that something remarkable was unfolding in the South, and we wanted to be on hand to witness it."

"Something remarkable" was, indeed, beginning to happen in the South.

A major Supreme Court decision had been made less than four months before Martin and Coretta moved to Montgomery. Many people believe that this decision led to the beginning of the civil rights movement. The court case began in the early 1950s, when an eight-year-old black girl named Linda Brown had to walk more than a mile each way between her home and school in Topeka, Kansas. She had to cross railroad tracks and go through a bad part of town—even though there was another elementary school, for white children, just a few blocks from her home. Linda's father, Oliver Brown, went to the school and asked to enroll his daughter.

Unlike many Southern states, Kansas had no law requiring black and white children to be separated. Still, the school principal said no. He insisted that it would be better for Linda to be with her own race.

Mr. Brown decided to go to court against the Topeka Board of Education. He argued that forcing black children to go to different schools made them feel inferior. The Board of Education, on the other hand, argued that the separation prepared black children for a life where they would often experience segregation. The court in Kansas listened to both sides. In the end, the judges decided that, yes, segregation in schools *is* unfair to black students. Amazingly, however, they sided with the Board of Education. The Supreme Court, they explained, had never overturned *Plessy v. Ferguson*, so they felt they must enforce the old "separate but equal" laws—whether they were fair or not.

Oliver Brown would not give up. *Brown v. Board of Education* went all the way to the highest court in the land—the same court that had legalized Jim Crow laws decades earlier. It took a few years, but eventually the Supreme Court justices came to a unanimous decision.

"We come then to the question presented," Chief Justice Earl Warren announced on May 17, 1954. "Does segregation of children in public schools solely on the basis of race . . . deprive the children of the minority group of equal educational opportunities? We believe that it does."

Separation of black and white students was declared unconstitutional. It would no longer be legal for schools to deny admission to students based on their skin color—not in Kansas, and not in the South. Even though the Supreme Court's ruling applied only to education, it was the beginning of the end of Jim Crow laws.

In the South, many racist white people were well aware of what this ruling would mean, and they were upset about it. A senator from Virginia immediately claimed that the Supreme Court had "overstepped its boundaries." He, along with many of the people he represented, felt that the federal government was sticking its nose into the rights of states. This was how Southern states had felt a century earlier. It was this feeling that had eventually led to the Civil War when Southern states no longer wanted to be part of the United States.

Many Southerners quickly formed organizations that vowed to fight desegregation to the bitter end. The law was not yet being enforced by the federal government, so those who opposed racially mixed schools continued to stand their ground. No matter what the

Supreme Court had said, they would not allow black students in *their* white schools. Before long, both black and white citizens who openly supported desegregation began to find crosses burning in their front yards—a threat from the feared Ku Klux Klan. Intimidation of blacks in order to "keep them in their place" was on the rise in the South. At the same time, many black people had reached their limits; they would no longer be quiet. This boldness was the "remarkable" thing that Martin Luther King, Jr. had said was beginning in the South.

While *Brown v. Board of Education* was a positive force that helped to spark the civil rights movement, a very sad, negative event also energized the movement.

Not long after the Supreme Court ruled in favor of desegregation, a fourteen-year-old black boy named Emmett Till was sent to visit his uncle in Money, Mississippi. Emmett had grown up in Chicago, so he had never experienced the type of racism that existed in Mississippi in 1955. Before he left Chicago, Emmett's mother had told him to mind his manners while in the South. Emmett was a happy, bright boy who made friends easily in spite of a bad stutter, and though he was a bit of a practical joker, he generally minded his manners. His mother telling him to watch his manners was nothing new, so he didn't think much about it.

Three days after arriving in Money, Emmett met some of his cousins and a group of other black young people at a small general store called Bryant's Grocery and Meat Market. The store was owned by a white couple, Carolyn and Roy Bryant. Although the Bryants were very racist, they were happy to accept money from the black children who came to their store every afternoon to buy candy and soda after working in the cotton fields. Carolyn Bryant, who was working alone in the store that afternoon, permitted only two black children at a time inside the store. The children were not allowed to spend much time in the store, to be out of Carolyn's sight, or to touch Carolyn's hand when giving her their money—they had to lay the coins on the counter.

What happened when Emmett went into the store is not known for certain. One of Emmett's cousins watched him through the window and later said that Emmett, not knowing any better, had placed his money directly into Carolyn's hand. However, the cousin had not seen Emmett do anything else that Carolyn might have objected to. What is known for certain is that when the young people were leaving,

Emmett turned back around and whistled at Carolyn Bryant, who was standing on the store's front steps. Emmett had probably done this to get laughs from his friends, but none of the children laughed. Instead, they looked terrified, warning Emmett to run home to his uncle's shack as fast as he could. Emmett just shrugged it off and grinned. It was only a harmless joke.

Very late that night, an angry pounding on the door of his uncle's shack awoke Emmett. Moments later, there was shouting. Emmett could tell that the two shouting voices were the voices of white men.

"I said we come here to teach that boy a lesson!" one of the men screamed furiously. "Where is he, old man?"

Shaking with terror, Emmett Till was dragged from his bed, thrown into the back of a pickup truck, and driven toward the Tallahatchie River. Before being thrown into the deep river with a 75-pound cotton-gin fan tied around his neck with barbed wire, Emmett was beaten with clubs, kicked, and shot in the head.

Three days later, Emmett's body was found. The fourteen-year-old was nearly unrecognizable; his nose had been completely flattened, his tongue was cut out, and one of his eyeballs hung halfway down his face. When the sheriff of the little Mississippi town saw Emmett's remains, he refused to allow the corpse to be returned to Emmett's mother in Chicago. Most likely, he was afraid that Mrs. Till would press charges. Only three hours before Emmett was to be buried without family, witnesses, or ceremony, Mrs. Till obtained a court order to have her son's corpse returned to Chicago. Angry and worried, the sheriff then ordered the casket to be sealed and padlocked so that it could not be reopened.

However, not only did Mrs. Till reopen the casket, she demanded that pictures be taken of her son's horribly disfigured face. And she insisted upon the casket being open at the funeral.

"Let the people see what I have seen," Mrs. Till said through tears. "I think everybody needs to know what had happened to Emmett Till."

Soon, the world would know what happened to Emmett Till, and this knowledge produced shock and outrage that fueled the already-growing fire of the civil rights movement.

Making the fire hotter was the trial of Till's murderers, Roy Bryant and his brother, J.W. Milam. Emmett's uncle testified that Bryant and his brother were the men who had taken

Emmett away in a truck that night. And the corpse recovered from the river was wearing a ring that had belonged to Emmett Till's father, a ring Emmett never took off. The all-white, all-male jury took only a few minutes to reach a verdict.

The jury concluded that there was no clear evidence to prove that the body found in the river was Emmett Till's.

Roy Bryant and his brother walked away, free men.

It was in these remarkable yet horrifying times that Martin and Coretta moved back to the South. Martin Luther King, Jr., sensed what was coming. The anger and frustration of black people in the United States had been simmering for more than 300 years. African Americans had endured slavery, lynching, humiliation.

"One realizes that eventually the cup of endurance runs over," King would later write about that time, "and human personality cries out, 'I can't take it no longer.'"

CHAPTER 4

"I'm going to preach on Sunday about how you deal with the problem of fear," Martin said to Coretta not long after they had moved to Montgomery, Alabama.

Martin was now the minister at the Dexter Avenue Baptist Church. It was a smaller church than his father's, but the people who attended Dexter were very dedicated to it. Dexter had been built right after the Civil War, during a period known as Reconstruction (1865–1877). This was a brief time in the South when freed slaves enjoyed the rare experience of fair treatment and, sometimes, even moderate wealth. Many lived and worked in the same neighborhoods as white people, and they built homes, businesses, and churches in town centers, which had previously been all-white.

Dexter was in the Montgomery town square, a strictly white area by 1955. Because the black neighborhoods had been pushed farther and farther away from the white neighborhoods in the center of town, many in Martin's congregation had to ride city buses for miles to get to church. No one complained about this, but it was hard on some of the elderly black women, who had to get up and stand in the back when a white man boarded the bus and wanted a seat. Young and old alike were afraid of arrest, humiliation, or worse if they fought against these rules that gave special privileges to white people.

Creating fear in the hearts and minds of black people was not just a tactic used by terror groups such as the Ku Klux Klan or by lynch mobs. Unfortunately, it was, all too often, used by city officials and police officers, too. Racists had fears of their own. They were very afraid of black people having rights, and they thought that threats and intimidation would keep blacks too afraid to fight for equality.

Fear. Martin knew that this was at the very core of hatred and racism. *Certainly,* he thought, *there must be a way of dealing with fear.* That Sunday, he looked out over his congregation, hoping to help them through these difficult times.

"We must unflinchingly face our fears," Martin explained. "This confrontation will, to some measure, grant us power. . . . We can master fear through one of the supreme virtues known to man—courage. Courage is the power of the mind to overcome fear."

And not long after Martin Luther King, Jr., delivered his sermon on fear, a most unlikely individual would present a cool, dignified display of courage rarely seen in Montgomery, Alabama, in 1955.

"Y'all better make it light on yourselves and let me have those seats," the burly white bus driver shouted back to four black passengers as four white passengers boarded the full bus. Three of the black passengers stood up and began moving to the back, but one, a forty-two-year-old seamstress named Rosa Parks, sat very still, staring out at the grey December evening.

"I said let me have those seats!" the driver said angrily, getting up to walk back toward Mrs. Parks. When he reached her, she calmly turned to look up at him glaring down at her.

"Why don't you stand up?" the driver asked, becoming more confused than angry at this point. No black person had ever refused to move.

"I don't think I should have to stand up," Rosa Parks said simply.

"Well, if you don't stand up, I'm going to call the police and have you arrested," the driver said, confident that his threat would scare her to the back of the bus.

Parks looked at the driver with no fear whatsoever and replied, "You may do that."

As Parks was pulled off the bus by a police officer, she asked him, "Why do you push us around?"

Perhaps the officer was a bit stunned to be questioned so bluntly by this small black woman. He shrugged his shoulders and admitted, "I don't know, but the law's the law."

Many years later, Rosa Parks would write about the night that she refused to stand up: "People always say that I didn't give up my seat because I was tired, but that isn't true. I was not tired physically, or no more tired than I usually was at the end of a working day. I was not old, although some people have an image of me as being old then. I was forty-two. No, the only tired I was, was tired of giving in."

Rosa Parks was not alone. Blacks all over the South and beyond were tired of giving in. The time had finally come. Through the seemingly simple act of refusing to give up a seat on a bus, the civil rights movement was born on

December 1, 1955. As Parks sat in her jail cell that Thursday night, Martin Luther King, Jr., received a call from a friend, E.D. Nixon, who was active in the Montgomery NAACP (National Association for the Advancement of Colored People). Nixon felt that the black community in Montgomery should protest Parks's arrest and the unfair seating laws by boycotting the buses. After all, most of the bus passengers were black. If they refused to ride the buses, the Montgomery public transit system would go bankrupt in time. The bus system would *have* to change the law if they wanted to remain in business.

Martin agreed that a boycott sounded like a good plan. Instantly, E.D. Nixon was asking Martin to help organize the boycott, hand out leaflets, and use his church as a meeting place for the community. Martin hesitated. He already had so many other responsibilities as a pastor. And, more important, Coretta had just given birth to their first child, Yolanda Denise, a month earlier. He wanted to spend *more* time at home, not less.

"Brother Nixon, let me think on it awhile, and call me back," Martin said.

But Nixon felt there was no time to spare. It was Friday evening, and he wanted the boycott to begin first thing Monday morning.

There was too much to do to allow Martin time to "think on it awhile." Nixon then called Ralph Abernathy. Abernathy was the pastor of the Montgomery First Baptist Church, and in the short time that Martin had lived in Montgomery, he and Abernathy had become very close friends. At age 29, Abernathy was a few years older than Martin, and Martin tended to look up to him and depend on him as he would a big brother. Nixon knew that if anyone could convince Martin to work on the bus boycott, it was Ralph Abernathy.

Nixon had been right. Abernathy convinced his friend that the boycott was not just another "responsibility." It was the start of something big. It would be the first time blacks had worked together peacefully to change an unfair law. History would be made, and Abernathy wanted Martin to be a part of it.

While speaking with Abernathy, Martin realized that what blacks in Montgomery would be doing was very similar to the nonviolent tactics that Gandhi had used.

"As I thought further, I came to see that what we were really doing was withdrawing our cooperation from an evil system, rather than merely withdrawing our support from the bus company," Martin would later write. "From that moment on, I thought of our movement as an act of massive noncooperation. From then on I rarely used the word 'boycott.'"

The next day, forty leaders of the Montgomery black community met at Dexter Avenue Baptist Church. Together, they came up with a plan for the boycott, agreeing that it should begin on Monday, December 5. Thousands and thousands of leaflets were printed: *Don't ride the bus to work, to town, to school, or any place Monday December 5. If you work, take a cab, or share a ride, or walk.* That Saturday night, King and Abernathy, along with other community leaders and dozens of young people, walked for miles, handing out the leaflets and spreading the word. People seemed enthusiastic, and everyone promised to stay off the buses.

However, King was worried. It was one thing for people to say they supported the boycott, but would they really participate? There had already been murmurings about the Ku Klux Klan taking violent action against those who participated in this "massive noncooperation."

Fear. King lay awake for a long time Sunday night, praying that courage would overcome fear the next morning.

"Martin, Martin, come quickly!" Coretta shouted from the front room of their house very early Monday morning. King rushed to the front room to find Coretta jumping with excitement and pointing out the window at a city bus.

"Darling, it's empty!" Coretta said, grabbing her husband's hand. Coretta and Martin stood at the window for nearly an hour as they watched buses roll by every ten minutes or so. Every single one was empty except for a few white passengers. King then hurried out to his car to pick up Abernathy. The two of them drove around Montgomery for hours, watching empty buses and full sidewalks.

"The sidewalks were crowded with laborers and domestic workers trudging patiently to their jobs and home again, sometimes as much as twelve miles," King later recalled. "They knew why they walked. . . . And as I watched them I knew that there is nothing more majestic than the determined courage of individuals willing to suffer and sacrifice for their freedom and dignity."

That afternoon, the group of black community leaders met again. They decided to form an organization to handle all the details of the boycott. The newly formed Montgomery Improvement Association (MIA) unanimously chose Martin Luther King, Jr., as its president. King's first duty as president would be to deliver an inspirational speech at a massive gathering of Montgomery's black population—in one hour! King was used to having an entire week to write his sermons. Nonetheless, he did not disappoint the 15,000 people who jammed the large Holt Street Church. As television cameras focused on him—and thousands of determined, brave African Americans looked to him—King knew that he was about to deliver the most important speech of his young life.

"My friends, there comes a time when people get tired of being trampled over by the iron feet of oppression. . . . We are not wrong in what we are doing. If we are wrong, the Supreme Court of this nation is wrong. If we are wrong, the Constitution of the United States is wrong. If we are wrong, God Almighty is wrong!"

King continued by pointing out that the boycott must remain peaceful and that their only weapon must be "the weapon of protest." After a long standing ovation for King's speech, Ralph Abernathy listed the three demands that must be met before the boycott would end: (1) Courteous treatment by bus drivers must be guaranteed. (2) Passengers would be seated on a first-come, first-served basis. (3) Black drivers must be hired for the routes in black areas of Montgomery.

When Abernathy finished reading the list, he explained that the boycott might take a while. It would mean many more days and miles of walking in the cold winter weather. It might mean harassment from racists. It could even mean danger. Then Abernathy asked for those who were in favor of continuing the boycott to stand up. All 15,000 people rose to their feet.

"That night was Montgomery's moment in history," King would later write.

"Listen, nigger, we've taken all we want from you. Before next week, you'll be sorry you ever came to Montgomery."

King was awakened in the middle of the night by a vicious phone call. As the boycott wore on and King became better known as the leader of Montgomery's black community, he also became the target of racist anger. Hate mail filled his mailbox. Death threats and curses were shouted at him when he walked down the city streets. Then, about a month after the boycott began, King's house was bombed while he was speaking at an MIA meeting.

Coretta and Yolanda had been home when the bomb exploded, but luckily they had been in a back room, and the damage was in the front part of the house. King rushed home to find an angry crowd of black people gathered outside.

They were shouting and swearing revenge on white people for the bombing. Some of them gripped broken bottles and waved knives and guns in the air. Martin Luther King, Jr., simply held up his hand to silence the crowd.

"We must meet hate with love," King said, shaking his head. "Please—put down your weapons and go home. We cannot solve this problem through retaliation. We must meet violence with nonviolence. . . . We must meet hate with love."

The white policemen who had responded to the bombing and who had stood nervously behind King on his front porch, heaved great sighs of relief when the angry crowd disappeared quietly into the night. One officer was reported to have reached for King's hand and, while shaking it heartily, said, "Thank you, Dr. King. You just saved our lives."

Much later that night, the ringing phone once again startled King out of a restless sleep.

"Look here, boy" an eerie whisper came through the receiver, "If you aren't out of this town in three days, we're gonna blow your brains out and blow up your house again."

King hung up quickly, his hands shaking with both anger and fear. He walked into the kitchen to make some coffee, knowing that there would be no more sleep for him that night. He put his head in his hands and prayed.

"Lord, I am at the end of my powers. I have nothing left. . . . I'm losing my courage. I can't face it alone."

As King would later tell it, a sudden sense of calm and peace came over him, and "an inner voice . . . the voice of Jesus" spoke to him, telling King that he must continue to stand up for what was right. The voice promised King that he would never be alone, even to the end of the world.

From that moment on, King moved forward with confidence and conviction. He would be afraid at times, but he would never again lose his courage or feel that he was alone in this struggle to change the world for the better.

King would need this new confidence.

First, Daddy King began pressuring his son to move back to Atlanta, calling the work that King was doing "wild and dangerous." Daddy King appeared at his son's door one night unannounced, having driven all the way from Atlanta.

"Better to be a live dog than a dead lion!" King's father bellowed as a greeting. Immediately, Daddy King launched into all the reasons why Martin should quit the dangerous work he was doing.

Daddy King and his son would argue until sunrise, but M.L. would not return to Atlanta. His path was set, and though he hated to fight with his father, he knew in his heart that he was doing the right thing.

Then, King and ninety other black community leaders were arrested for violating a very old anti-boycott law. Essentially, it was a law that was no longer enforced, but the city decided to dig it up in order to arrest the leaders of the boycott. City officials believed this would destroy the boycott's momentum. In fact, it had just the opposite effect. Reporters from all over the country flocked to Montgomery to cover this unusual event as the city jails filled with black leaders. As King fought for equality, he had never wanted to become a celebrity, but now his face was on television and in newspapers. When the city realized that jailing the black leaders was only adding strength to the boycott, they released everyone.

The Montgomery city authorities refused to change any of the unfair bus laws, however. For months, neither the city authorities nor the black leaders backed down. When a federal court ruled that bus segregation was unlawful, the city authorities instantly appealed the court's decision to a higher level. This would extend the boycott for months—and already it was driving the bus company nearly into bankruptcy.

The city assumed that blacks would now give up. After all, they had already been walking, taking taxis, and carpooling for half a year. Some even rode mules or drove horses and buggies to town. Surely, the authorities thought, the black community would now give up this silly fight over bus seats.

But the black community would not give up. Every single person protesting knew that this fight was about far more than seats on a bus; it was about dignity and fair treatment. And so, through a harsh winter, through springtime downpours, and into the blazing Alabama summer heat, the black citizens of Montgomery refused to ride the buses. When, in frustration, the city officials declared carpooling illegal, more people walked. Then, when the city created a ruling against use of taxis as "mass transportation" and would not allow blacks to use them, more people walked.

King often held mass meetings at the larger churches, and he gave inspiring speeches that comforted and lifted the spirits of the thousands of protestors who came to hear him speak. To blacks in Montgomery, he had truly become their leader and a hero. At the end of one meeting, an elderly black woman approached King shyly. She explained that she had to walk to and from her job as a cleaning woman every day, but she was proud to be part of the boycott.

"I'm not walking for myself. I'm walking for my children and my grandchildren," she said, reaching out to grasp King's hand. "My feets is tired, but my soul is rested."

CHAPTER 5

The bus boycott wore on much longer than anyone had ever imagined. The city of Montgomery stubbornly refused to give in to the demands of the black community. As the boycott pushed through the summer and into the next winter, the 42,000 black residents of Montgomery faithfully continued walking and sharing rides. Many racist white people grew angry and frustrated. *How can they not give up?* the white people wondered. *How is it possible that their strength and pride continue to grow stronger?* they asked one another.

Some whites did everything they could think of to break the spirits of the protestors. Police officers began arresting black citizens for the smallest and most insignificant reasons. Even exceeding the speed limit by only a few miles might result in a night or two in jail. If blacks complained, police would increase their fines or, in some cases, use physical force to get their point across. The police were especially likely to pull over cars that appeared to contain black carpoolers.

Blacks were yelled at, spit on, and pelted with rocks and garbage as they walked to and from their jobs or their schools. Still, the black community maintained its dignity, never once lashing back in violence. This only made racist whites more furious. Terror groups began setting off more bombs at the homes of black leaders and in black churches. Again, the black citizens continued to protest peacefully with increased determination. In desperation, a Montgomery newspaper published a false story saying that the boycott was over. However, King had learned about the story the evening before it was to be printed, so he and several other boycott organizers spent most of that night traveling around town and warning blacks not to ride the buses the next morning, regardless of what they read in the paper.

Then, preying on the religious faith of the black community, some whites tried to convince the protestors that they were sinners for causing such a disruption. How dare they put a company out of business and force people out of jobs just so they could have better seats!

At a mass meeting during this time, King spoke to the thousands gathered. He had just been released from jail after his second arrest. With a little grin, he began, "Tonight I stand before you, a convicted minister." The crowd laughed and cheered.

"I seem to have committed three sins," King continued. "I have done three things that are wrong. First of all, being born a Negro. . . . Second, being tired of segregation. I have committed the sin of being tired of the injustices and discriminations heaped upon us. Third, having the moral courage to sit up and express our tiredness. That is my third sin."

The crowd stood and clapped for King for a long time. As King looked across the 3,000 protestors gathered that night, he knew that no matter how many months the boycott would last, the black community would not give up or give in. "We stand in life at midnight," King would later write about the struggle, "we are always on the threshold of a new dawn."

That new dawn finally broke. On November 13, 1956, the United States Supreme Court ruled that segregation of buses was unconstitutional. That evening, 8,000 black protestors gathered to hear King announce the long-awaited news. It would be another month until the Supreme Court would enforce the new law in Montgomery, but the victory was celebrated that evening.

On December 21, more than a year after Rosa Parks had refused to move, the boycott came to an end. The first black man to board a Montgomery bus and sit in a front seat was Martin Luther King, Jr. As the bus pulled up, the black driver opened the door while camera crews from all over the country filmed the momentous event. The driver smiled and asked, "Is that you, Dr. King?" King nodded, and the driver took off his hat in a show of respect. "Glad to have you with us this morning," he said. And with that, it was, as King would recall, "a glorious daybreak to end a long night of enforced segregation."

However, while the law may have changed, racism had not. In fact, the new law only inflamed racists' anger.

"If you allow the niggers to go back to the buses and sit on the front seat, we are going to burn down more than fifty nigger houses in one night," a caller screamed through the phone to King the evening following King's historic ride in the front seat. Then, in the days and months that followed, violence rose. Snipers shot at buses. A number of black homes were bombed, including Ralph Abernathy's, and an unexploded bomb was found on King's front porch one morning. Then the Ku Klux Klan went on a rampage, riding in truckloads through black neighborhoods while yelling obscenities and threats, and burning crosses in front yards.

But something had changed. Blacks no longer cowered or hid when the Klan drove through. Now, blacks came out to sit on their porches and watch as though a parade of clowns was passing by. Some blacks even waved and laughed at the Klansmen in their white robes and ridiculous pointed hats.

The Ku Klux Klan tried in vain to frighten blacks the way they had only a year earlier, but "it seemed to have lost its spell," King later wrote. ". . . One cold night, a small Negro boy was seen warming his hands at a burning cross."

King had been right two years earlier: "Something remarkable" was indeed happening in the South.

In the months following the bus victory in Montgomery, several other cities in the South followed Montgomery's example. In cities like Birmingham, Alabama, and Tallahassee, Florida, black leaders began organizing peaceful protests against segregated busing. As expected, racists lashed out violently against the idea of black people having equal rights. And sometimes, frustrated and angry blacks fought back.

King, Abernathy, and other ministers and leaders in Montgomery closely watched these new bus boycotts develop. King was troubled by the occasional violence by blacks, so he and other leaders decided to form an organization that would serve blacks throughout the South. The organization would offer spiritual guidance, funding, and training for peaceful protest. Like the National Association for the Advancement of Colored People, it would be a civil rights organization.

Black ministers and community leaders from ten Southern states met to form this organization. They decided to name it the Southern Christian Leadership Conference (SCLC). At first, they had wanted to call it "Negro Leaders Conference on Nonviolent Integration," but worried that the name was both too long and too confusing. After all, they hoped that this new group would eventually move beyond issues of integration. In addition, the group did not want its name to attract the attention of racists who might become abusive. They hoped that the word *Christian* in the name would lead racists to assume that this was just a harmless group of black preachers.

King was elected president of the SCLC, and his fame, influence, and importance continued to build. In February of 1957, King's picture was on the cover of *Time* magazine. Now, people around the world knew King's face, his story, and his commitment. And in the southern United States, more and more black people were beginning to see him as something of a miracle worker. As King traveled, giving speeches to motivate and inspire blacks, huge crowds watched him with obvious awe. "When King comes in," one newspaper reporter wrote, "you can hear a pin drop."

King was never comfortable with a lot of praise and attention. He was eager to do the work needed to help blacks in the United States, but he was very reluctant to be looked upon as a hero or as anything more than a man with a desire to help others. Coretta, recalling that time, later wrote, "He would say to me, 'I am really disturbed about how fast all this has happened to me. People will expect me to perform miracles for the rest of my life. I don't want to be the kind of man who hits his peak at twenty-seven. . . . '"

Still, King moved forward, trying his best to disregard the growing number of reporters, crowds, and police officers that awaited him everywhere he went. One of the first things

King and the SCLC wanted to do was meet with President Dwight D. Eisenhower. No United States President had ever met with black leaders to discuss civil rights. King felt the time for a president to face the problems of blacks in the United States was overdue. However, Eisenhower ignored the requests for meetings, both with King and with the SCLC.

Then, in the fall of 1957, even though Eisenhower still chose to ignore King, he found that he could no longer keep his back turned on the growing civil rights movement.

Many states in the South were very slow to enforce desegregation on city buses. Usually, desegregation was met with a great deal of bitterness and resentment. And even though the *Brown v. Board of Education* ruling had been made more than three years earlier, schools throughout the South remained fiercely segregated. It was one thing for the Supreme Court to make important decisions, but it was quite another to get states to enforce the laws behind those decisions.

Whites made very clear that they would make conditions miserable for any black students who demanded admission to all-white schools. For a while, the threats and intimidation worked, but in September of 1957, nine black high school students in Little Rock, Arkansas, refused to back down.

The evening before the students were going to try for the third time to enter all-white Central High School, Arkansas's governor, Orval Faubus, said that if the students followed through with their plan, "blood will run in the streets." Two earlier times, the black students, known as the "Little Rock Nine," had been turned away from the school when angry mobs had screamed, spit, and thrown rocks on them. One of the nine, a sixteen-year-old girl, had even had acid thrown in her face. Still, in the spirit of King's nonviolent action, the nine young people had never returned one angry word. They had held their heads high and endured the mistreatment with dignity and silence.

Faubus's plan to call in the Arkansas National Guard to block the Little Rock Nine from entering Central High prompted President Eisenhower to get involved. Eisenhower warned the governor that refusing the black students entry was now against the law and that he must not do it. Furthermore, Eisenhower firmly told Governor Faubus that he must also protect the students from the angry mobs at the school's entrance.

Faubus, probably more concerned about keeping his job than about anything else, backed down. However, he did little to help protect the

Little Rock Nine from being attacked the next morning. Instead of using the National Guard, Faubus sent a few police officers to the school. The police were overwhelmed by the rioting crowd of racists, and once again the nine black students were sent home.

The President had had enough. The next day, he ordered both the 101st Airborne Division of the United States Army and the entire Arkansas National Guard to surround Central High and escort the nine black students into the school. Finally, amid screaming crowds, helicopters, sirens, and soldiers with loaded rifles, the Little Rock Nine entered the school. Around the country, people watched the news coverage and shook their heads.

"It didn't make sense to me then, and it doesn't now," one of the nine, Minnijean Brown, said in an interview in 1997. "I am never going to say it made sense."

It was, perhaps, the utter senselessness of the shouting racists contrasted with the calm dignity of the nine young people that moved the nation. And it was not just people outside the South who were shocked by what they saw. Many white Southerners also found Faubus's racism to be disgusting and ignorant. It was embarrassing, and, most important, it was a vivid example of just how cruel racism was.

As a result, many white Southerners became determined to help change the unfair treatment of blacks in the South.

More than fifty years later, the day that the Little Rock Nine entered Central High School is still considered one of the most important events of the civil rights movement.

The events in Little Rock reminded Martin Luther King, Jr., just how much work there was to do. In particular, he began thinking about how desperately important it was for black Americans in the South to register to vote. Until they did, people in political power, like Faubus, would continue to get elected and would continue to make life difficult for blacks.

However, in many Southern areas, white people often made registering to vote nearly impossible for blacks. Some blacks were forced to take unfair voter registration tests that whites knew they wouldn't pass. Sometimes when blacks walked into an office to register, officials claimed that the office was closed or out of forms, or that the workers were out to lunch or too busy. Many black people in the South had simply given up trying to register to vote.

King discussed this problem with the Southern Christian Leadership Conference.

"The chief weapon in our fight for civil rights is the vote," he said during a meeting of leaders. "I can foresee the Negro vote becoming the decisive vote in national elections."

Everyone agreed, and the SCLC decided to launch what they referred to as a "Crusade for Citizenship." During this crusade, King and the members of the SCLC were determined to help blacks in the South understand the importance of their vote and the process of registration. Also, the SCLC wanted to make President Eisenhower aware of the deceitful, illegal tricks that were used to keep blacks from registering. King knew that none of this would be easy. Blacks were suspicious of the government and elections, and Eisenhower continued to ignore King's requests to meet.

While King worked tirelessly as both a minister and a leader in the civil rights movement, his second child, Martin Luther III, was born near the end of 1957. In the months that followed his son's birth, King was often sad when he thought about all he was missing at home with his two babies. Throughout 1958, King was away from home more than he was there. Now a world-famous activist, King received hundreds of requests for appearances. In 1958 alone, he delivered 208 speeches and traveled more than 780,000 miles, including a trip to Ghana, Africa.

Back home in Montgomery late in 1958, King one day made an appointment to speak with his lawyer about some legal questions. Coretta was glad to have a chance to spend some time with her husband, and decided to accompany him to the county courthouse, where the lawyer worked. As Coretta and Martin waited in the lobby of the courthouse, a police officer glared at King, recognizing him right away. Immediately, the officer marched over to King and told him to leave or risk getting arrested for loitering.

"But I am waiting to see my lawyer, Fred Gray," King responded calmly and politely.

"If you don't get the hell out of here, you're going to *need* a lawyer!" the police officer snarled.

King did not move. He didn't argue, but he didn't move. He simply stared, with no expression, at the officer.

"Boy, you done it now," the policeman said and yelled for another officer to help him. The two officers painfully twisted King's arms behind his back and roughly led him down the stairs and out the door toward City Hall. Coretta followed behind. When she begged the officers not to hurt her husband, one whirled around and barked, "You want to go to jail too, girl? Just nod your head if you want to!"

"Don't say anything, darling!" King said, wincing as the officers kicked him for speaking.

As the policemen pushed and kicked King along the sidewalk toward the county jail, his followers and admirers, both black and white, gathered and watched in alarm. Then the alarm turned to anger. Some began shouting threats of retaliation as they chased after King and the policemen. King simply turned toward the crowd and raised a hand and shook his head. It was a gesture some had seen before, and they knew what it meant. Nothing good could come from repaying violence with violence.

"The beauty of nonviolence," King would later write, "is that it seeks to break the chain reaction of evil."

CHAPTER 6

"The time has come when I should no longer accept bail," King said to Coretta. "If I commit a crime in the name of civil rights, I will go to jail and serve the time."

After being roughed up a bit, King had been released from jail, and a court date was set for his trial. King knew in advance that he would probably be charged with disobeying an officer. He knew that he would have the option of either paying a fine or spending time in jail, and now he had decided to take the jail time. Coretta was upset with this decision. For black men, time spent in a Southern jail could be exceedingly dangerous. Sometimes black prisoners simply disappeared with no explanation at all.

Still, Coretta understood why her husband was making this choice. Following in the footsteps of Gandhi, King knew that a person must suffer for the cause he or she believes in. King could not simply write a check to avoid the discomforts of standing up for his beliefs. Gandhi had been thrown into prison many times during his years of nonviolent protest, and now King was ready to go to prison as well. A year earlier during the bus boycott in Montgomery, King had told a crowd that blacks in the South were "in for a season of suffering." That season had begun.

King knew that whenever he was put in jail, his arrest made headlines around the world. He also knew that nothing helped the cause of civil rights more than exposing the meanness of racists. He realized, for example, that when a Southern judge tossed a respected leader like King into jail for the "crime" of waiting for his lawyer, the world would respond in outrage. King knew that going to jail was one of the best things he could do for the cause.

However, things did not go as King had planned. After he chose jail time over paying the fine, King waited in line for the bus that would take him to a cell for two weeks. Suddenly, a police officer pulled him out of line and told him to go home; his fine had been paid. That evening, King found out that the Montgomery police commissioner was the one who had paid the fine. Like King, the commissioner was well aware of the huge amount of publicity that the civil rights movement would receive if King went to jail. The commissioner's sarcastic explanation, however, was that he was trying "to save taxpayers the expense of feeding King for fourteen days."

"Mrs. King, I want you to prepare yourself. I have some bad news for you."

One evening in the fall of 1958, a phone call from a doctor in New York City came in just as Coretta was putting the children to bed. Coretta sat down, her hands shaking. She had long feared the day that she would receive a call telling her that Martin had been killed. After all, death threats arrived in the mail nearly every day. Was this that call?

The doctor quickly explained that King was alive, but he was in very serious condition. King had been in New York autographing his first book, *Stride Toward Freedom*, a book about the Montgomery bus boycott. A long line of people had waited for a quick autograph and, perhaps, a word or two from Dr. King. Barely having a chance to look up as he signed his name, King did the best he could to answer questions politely.

Finally, near the end of the line, a woman simply asked, "Are you Dr. King?"

"Yes, I am," King said, his head still down.

"Luther King," the woman said in a low voice, "I've been after you for five years."

At the very moment King looked up, the woman, a forty-two-year-old black woman named Izola Curry, pulled out a long, sharp letter opener and plunged it into King's chest. Immediately, there was screaming and confusion all around, but King sat very still, staring down at the handle of the sharp blade. He was rushed to Harlem Hospital. King was not in a lot of pain, but he had to wait for three long hours before doctors could remove the letter opener. It took them that long to decide exactly how to go about such a delicate operation.

"Days later," King wrote in his autobiography, " . . . [the doctor] told me that the razor tip of the instrument had been touching my aorta and that my whole chest had to be opened to extract it. 'If you had sneezed during all those hours of waiting,' Dr. Maynard said, 'your aorta would have been punctured and you would have drowned in your own blood.'"

The woman who had stabbed King was mentally ill and did not even understand her own actions. Although she was arrested, King refused to press any charges against her, explaining quietly that he felt only sympathy for her and hoped that she would get the help she needed. It was important to King to apply the same peaceful and nonviolent actions to his personal life that he used in protests. Others urged King to sue the woman, to make sure she went to prison for life, but, as always, retaliation was something that King avoided. He believed that bringing more sorrow to a sick woman would help no one.

As King lay recovering in the hospital, hundreds and hundreds of cards poured in from other civil rights organizers, politicians, and even important leaders of other countries. However, the card that meant the most to King was from a fourteen-year-old girl who wrote:

Dear Dr. King:

I am a ninth-grade student at White Plains High School. While it shouldn't matter, I would like to mention that I'm a white girl. I read in the paper of your misfortune and of your suffering. And I read that if you had sneezed you would have died. I'm simply writing to say that I'm so happy that you didn't sneeze.

King often referred to that letter in speeches and sermons, commenting with a grin that he, too, was so glad he hadn't sneezed that day.

After King was released from the hospital, he needed a few more weeks of recuperation. He was free to travel, though his doctors advised him against doing stressful or difficult work. This seemed, then, the perfect time for something that King had wanted to do for years: travel to India, the land of his mentor, Mahatma Gandhi.

Martin and Coretta spent three weeks in India, visiting many of the areas where Gandhi had lived and worked. They also spent quite a bit of time with India's prime minister, who took them to Gandhi's burial site, where King solemnly placed a wreath of flowers on the tomb. While King was impressed by the spirituality and peacefulness of the Indian people, he was disturbed by how much poverty there was.

"How can one avoid being depressed when he discovers that of India's 400 million people, more than 365 million make an annual income of less than sixty dollars?" King would later write.

In the bigger cities, the streets were full of starving homeless people. King thought about how, in America, a million dollars a day was spent just to store surplus food. "I know where we can store that food free of charge," he said to Coretta one evening, "in the wrinkled stomachs of the millions of people who go to bed hungry at night."

Throughout his travels, King observed how Indians were divided into different groups, known as "castes," based upon how much money they had. At the very bottom of this grouping system were the people who were so poor that they had no caste at all. Those people were known as "untouchables." Before Gandhi's peaceful protest against such discrimination, untouchables had very few rights and were separated from the upper castes. If untouchables attempted to associate or mingle with the upper classes, they were often beaten severely and sometimes killed.

Gandhi had worked very hard to do away with the caste system, sometimes fasting nearly to death in order to show how deeply he believed in this cause. To the shock of the upper castes, Gandhi even adopted a baby girl whose parents had been untouchables. In time, the young girl grew into a wise, kind, and beautiful woman. It was, perhaps, one of the more vivid examples of how ridiculous it was to treat people differently based on their wealth.

Those in the upper castes grew ashamed of their own prejudices when they saw that this young woman was, after all, no different from their own daughters.

Finally, laws were passed making it illegal to mistreat untouchables or to deny them their human rights. Nonviolent protest had worked. Sadly, however, laws did not change the behavior of many narrow-minded Indians in the upper classes. The poorest people continued to be mistreated even after Gandhi's death.

King could not help but see how much the situation of blacks in America was like that of the untouchables in India. When he returned to the United States, King was more determined than ever to continue on Gandhi's path of nonviolence. Perhaps the caste system had not yet disappeared in India, but Gandhi had revealed how shameful it was. He had changed the minds and hearts of millions of Indians. And he had done it all peacefully.

"Gandhi resisted evil with as much power as the violent resister," King would later reflect, "but he resisted with love instead of hate."

In 1959, King had a tough decision to make. After returning from India, he continued his book tour, signing copies of *Stride Toward Freedom*, and making speeches in support of the civil right movement. Additionally, the Southern Christian Leadership Conference had moved its headquarters to Atlanta. More and more frequently, King was not in Montgomery on Sunday to deliver a sermon to his congregation at Dexter Avenue Baptist Church. King struggled with the guilt of being an absent minister. He began to question whether he should resign from Dexter, move back to Atlanta, and devote all his time to helping blacks in the South. Finally, King made up his mind.

"History has thrust upon me a responsibility from which I cannot turn away," King told his congregation in a farewell sermon on November 29, 1959. He explained that he could not be "four or five men in one." King was sad to leave his church and so many friends, but he was relieved to know that he would now have more time to focus on the civil rights movement.

Martin, Coretta, and their two young children moved into a large rental house in Atlanta, just down the street from Daddy King's Ebenezer Baptist Church, and King agreed to help with pastor duties at Ebenezer whenever he had enough time. However, King was mostly interested in meeting with other leaders to decide what the SCLC should work on next.

Before King and his group had a chance to plan their course of action, however, a new form of protest in North Carolina demanded their attention.

"We don't serve colored here," the waiter behind the Woolworth's lunch counter in Greensboro, North Carolina, snapped at four black college students. "If you want to be served anything to eat or drink, you'll have to stand."

The students had been buying school supplies when they walked over to sit down on the stools at the counter and have coffee. Only white people were allowed to sit on the stools or in the booths. The students were well aware of this unfair rule, and for some time they had been planning to break it. When the waiter refused to serve them, the four students calmly responded that they would continue to sit at the counter until they were served. They sat quietly until the store closed. Some white people glared at the students, but one elderly white woman walked over, put her hands on two of the young men's shoulders and said, "Boys, I am so proud of you. You should have done this ten years ago."

The next morning, twenty-seven black students showed up and refused to move from the counter. As the four had done the day before, they all sat quietly, waiting for the service they never received. Four days later, more than 300 students jammed the Woolworth's lunch counter in this new form of peaceful protest. Soon, news of the students' refusal to move had swept the nation, and this same kind of protest, known as a "sit-in," began taking place all over the South. Typically, the sit-ins were conducted by high school and college students.

The young black people who participated in the sit-ins had to endure hours of boredom as they sat at "white only" counters, sometimes for entire days. Worse, however, was the taunting and abuse from racists who flocked to the restaurants where blacks sat. It was not uncommon for sit-in participants to be burned with cigarettes, covered with milkshakes and Coke, and pelted with food. For the most part, the protestors refused to fight back, following the nonviolent approach that King encouraged. Still, tempers flared from time to time when the young people felt they had put up with enough harassment.

As the sit-ins grew in popularity, and more and more college-aged people became active in civil rights, a new organization was formed: the Student Nonviolent Coordinating Committee (SNCC). SNCC focused on student protests at many of the "public" facilities that, since they did not allow blacks, were not really public at all. Libraries, parks, and swimming pools were added to lunch counters as places where blacks simply sat down, refusing to obey the unfair and outdated rules. Sometimes, whites responded by closing the facilities altogether, preferring to stubbornly deny even *themselves* rather than share anything with black people. But, more frequently, the protests led to changing the rules.

In Atlanta, SNCC looked to Martin Luther King, Jr., for support as they prepared to conduct a sit-in at a lunch counter in a Rich's department store. They asked King to join them, certain that he would be enthusiastic. However, King hesitated at first. The older generation of blacks, the generation Daddy King belonged to, frowned upon the sit-ins. They thought sit-ins would serve only to make white people angry and eventually lead to more, not fewer, problems. Daddy King repeatedly told his son that race problems should be solved in court, not in the streets or in places of business.

As always, King did not want to displease his father, but after much thought, he agreed to join the students on October 19, 1960, at the Rich's lunch counter, claiming, "I felt a moral obligation to be in it with them."

That morning, King and nearly 100 students sat down at the counter. Immediately, police stormed in and arrested all the sit-in participants for trespassing. This time, King was determined to remain in jail and neither post bail nor pay a fine.

"I would stay and serve the time if it was one year, five, or ten years," King later wrote. "And of course the students agreed to stay also."

When five days had passed and not one protestor had posted bail, many officials and residents of Atlanta began to get nervous. Already, the media was zeroing in on the jailed civil rights leader, Martin Luther King, Jr. Finally, on the sixth day, Rich's dropped all charges, and the mayor of Atlanta announced that he would work with merchants to put an end to segregation at restaurants. The students cheered as they were released from the jail, and King smiled as he looked forward to returning home to his wife and children.

Suddenly, however, King's smile vanished.

As the protestors filed out and signed release forms, King was grabbed by the arm. Officers informed him that he was still under arrest for violating the terms of a prior arrest. Months earlier, King had been given a ticket for driving with an Alabama license instead of a Georgia license, a minor traffic violation. Though King had paid the fine, police insisted that he was still under a suspended sentence, and that now he was in serious trouble.

King was thrown back into a jail cell and told that his punishment would be imprisonment and four months of hard labor. In the middle of the night, officers came to transfer him to a prison hundreds of miles away from Atlanta. No one would tell King where they were going.

"On the way there, they dealt with me just like I was some hardened criminal," King recalled. "They had me chained all the way down to my legs, and they tied my legs to something in the floor so there would be no way for me to escape."

Finally, the officers and King arrived at their destination—Reidsville State Prison, a remote facility deep in the heart of Klan country. This was the kind of prison where black prisoners simply disappeared and were never heard from again.

King's heart raced as he was led to a dark cell in the back corner of the prison. As he wrapped his fingers around the prison bars, his hands shook. For the first time, young Martin Luther King, Jr., feared for his life.

CHAPTER 7

"They are going to kill him. I know they are going to kill him!"

A panicked Coretta Scott King, not knowing who to turn to, placed a call to a very important United States senator, hoping that he would be able to get her husband's sentence reversed. He was unable to take the call, but one of his assistants assured Mrs. King that the senator would call her back right away. That senator was John F. Kennedy.

When Kennedy called Coretta back, he let her know how concerned he was about King's situation and that he was thinking of Coretta, who was pregnant with a third child. However, he refused to get directly involved in the matter. It was late October of 1960, and Kennedy was running for President against Richard Nixon. With the election only two weeks away,

Kennedy feared losing the millions of votes of white people in the South who would be angry if he helped King.

Still, Kennedy contacted his brother, Robert, a powerful lawyer, and asked him to call the judge in the case. Robert Kennedy was eager to help. He was furious that King had been imprisoned for such flimsy reasons.

"I don't know what he said in that conversation with the judge," King would later write, "but I was released the next day."

News of John F. Kennedy's call to Coretta reached the press, and, in the end, it cost him the votes of many white Southerners anyway. On the other hand, Kennedy's concern and his brother's help impressed many black voters. Blacks had typically voted for Republican presidential candidates ever since Republican Abraham Lincoln had freed the slaves during the Civil War. Now, many of them switched parties.

Although Martin Luther King, Jr., never publically endorsed either Kennedy or Nixon, Daddy King did. Before the Kennedys' calls to Coretta and the judge, Daddy King had vowed that he would never vote for a Democratic presidential nominee. He had been set on casting his vote for Nixon in 1960, but now he stood before his congregation at Ebenezer a week before the election and shouted, "If I had a suitcase full of votes, I'd take them all and place them at Senator Kennedy's feet!"

Daddy King felt that the Kennedys had saved his son's life. He would vote Democrat for the rest of his days. The following week, Kennedy beat Nixon by a very slim margin— only about 100,000 votes. Though Kennedy had originally feared that helping King would hurt his election chances, in the end it may, in fact, have won him the race.

Like the bus boycotts, the sit-in demonstrations had worked. Across the South, restaurants and lunch counters were becoming desegregated. However, other old Jim Crow laws still lingered in parts of the South, even though the Supreme Court had ruled against such racist laws. Blacks had learned that the only way to get fairness enforced was to demand it through demonstration. So, in May of 1961, a new form of peaceful demonstration began.

For years, it had been illegal to separate blacks from whites on trains, on interstate buses, or in waiting rooms of train and bus stations. Still, in many parts of the South, whites were unwilling to obey or enforce the law. Finally, a black man named James Farmer came up with a plan. He, along with thirteen other people (seven black and six white) decided to ride Greyhound and Trailways buses from Washington, D.C., through several Southern states, and end the journey with a rally in New Orleans. Along the way, the blacks would sit in the "whites only" section of the buses and the waiting rooms, while the whites would sit in the "colored only" sections. If asked to move, they would refuse.

"This was not civil disobedience really," Farmer later explained, "because we would be doing merely what the Supreme Court said we had a right to do. We felt we could count on the racists of the South to create a crisis so that the federal government would have to enforce the law."

Farmer expected there to be violence along the way, possibly even deaths. The thirteen riders, who would come to be known as the "Freedom Riders," trained for weeks, learning how to resist peacefully and how to avoid becoming violent themselves if they were attacked. Farmer, like King, was a close follower of Gandhi. He knew that the Freedom Riders would have to endure violence without retaliation if they were to be successful.

The first Freedom Ride was surprisingly nonviolent. A few Riders were arrested, and there was a scuffle in North Carolina, but, otherwise, things went smoothly. The Freedom Riders were pleased with how easy it had been to change the Jim Crow laws throughout Georgia. Perhaps, they thought, making these changes would not be difficult at all. Perhaps the South was ready for change after all.

It was not.

As the Freedom Riders moved farther south, two men in Birmingham, Alabama, made plans to have the Riders viciously attacked. Shockingly, these two men were a police sergeant, Tom Cook, and a safety commissioner, Eugene "Bull" Connor. Both men had close connections to the Ku Klux Klan, and they decided that it was time for these annoying Freedom Rides to end. Connor and Cook actually gave permission to the Klan to attack the Riders "for fifteen minutes" when they reached the small town of Anniston, not far from Birmingham. If the Freedom Riders did not give up, the attack in Birmingham would be worse.

"Yes, in Anniston, Alabama, when the first Freedom Rider bus arrived, there was a mob of men, white men, several hundred, standing there at the bus terminal waiting for the bus," Farmer recalled in a 1985 interview. "And the members of the mob had their weapons in plain evidence, pistols, guns, blackjacks, clubs, chains, knives. . . . "

Farmer and the other Riders decided it would be suicide to get off the bus, so they told the driver to continue to Birmingham. But while they were stopped at the Anniston station, the mob of racists slashed the tires, forcing the bus to stop again when several tires went flat on a lonely two-lane road. The mob of Klansmen had been following close behind in cars and trucks. The mob surrounded the bus, throwing rocks and cement blocks through its windows. Finally, a small bomb was thrown into the bus, setting it on fire. Two men in the mob blocked the bus doors, hoping to burn all the Freedom Riders alive. When a fuel tank exploded, however, the mob backed off, and the Riders escaped. Only the warning shots of a passing highway patrolman kept the mob from beating the Riders to death as they fled the burning bus.

The Freedom Riders refused to give up. Those who were not too injured to continue, boarded another bus and headed to Birmingham. When the bus pulled into the station, the mob closed in again. As the Freedom Riders bravely stepped out, they were instantly slammed with bats, tire irons, rocks, and bicycle chains. White Riders were beaten the worst, as the racists were particularly infuriated that anyone white would actually help a black person obtain his or her rights. Also viciously attacked were the media, and especially photographers. As always, racists were angry and frustrated that the civil rights movement was receiving so much attention— and the sympathy of the world.

"This was the biggest news of the day," Farmer pointed out. "It monopolized the television news every evening and the headlines of newspapers—not only in this country, but in Asia, in Africa, and in Europe."

At home in Atlanta, Martin Luther King, Jr., watched the progress of the Freedom Riders with both pride and anger. He admired the restraint of the Riders; though they had been beaten bloody, not one Rider had lifted a fist or a voice in anger. Still, King was furious that such violence had been heaped upon people who were simply asking for the most basic of human rights. He worried that the spirit of the Riders was being so brutally worn down that it was only a matter of time until the Freedom Riders fought back. Then, King thought anxiously, the violence would erupt in an explosive chain reaction throughout the South.

The Freedom Riders were scheduled to arrive in Montgomery on May 20, 1961, so King decided to be there to greet them. He also planned to hold a mass rally at Ralph

Abernathy's church to honor the Riders. He wanted the Riders to know how important their work was and how much everyone appreciated and admired their nonviolent approach.

That evening, 1,200 people, both black and white, crammed into the First Baptist Church. There was joyous singing from the crowd and inspiring words from both King and Abernathy. But even as the 1,200 bowed their heads to pray for the continued strength of the Freedom Riders, hundreds of carloads of racists began arriving from the surrounding towns and countryside. With eerie silence, the mob of thousands gathered around the church, and then, as the refrain of "We Shall Overcome" echoed inside, the mob outside began hurling rocks at the stained glass windows. Splinters of glass fell on those gathered in the church, and through the broken windows, King and others could see that cars were being set on fire.

King and Abernathy calmed the people in the church and assured them that everything would be all right. "Fear not," King shouted. "We've come too far to turn back!" But King was deeply worried. He could tell from the yelling outside that the mob was huge, and it had completely surrounded the church. The 1,200 people were trapped. Canisters of tear gas whizzed through the windows, and a small bomb landed near one of King's aides. Luckily, it did not explode. Hours later, in desperation, King and Abernathy went to the church basement, and King called Robert Kennedy, who was now Attorney General of the United States. Kennedy had helped King before—perhaps he would help him again.

Kennedy had already heard about the situation in Montgomery. "Seven hundred U.S. marshals have already been dispatched," Kennedy assured King. In the end, however, both the marshals and the National Guard were needed to break up the dangerous mob. The 1,200 gathered at the church were not able to leave until 4:30 in the morning. Later, Coretta would recall, "It was a night of horror, and it was very discouraging because it revealed the irrationality and cruelty of racism."

About 250 miles southwest of Atlanta, in a part of the South that was considered to be the very heart of racism, was the small town of Albany, Georgia. Members of Student Nonviolent Coordinating Committee had traveled to Albany to make some changes—and there were a lot of changes to be made. In Albany, all of the old Jim Crow laws were still firmly in place. Buses, lunch counters, schools, parks, and even movie theaters were still segregated.

As the young people of SNCC began protesting in Albany and pushing for change, they were thrown into jail by the dozens. Soon, a hundred SNCC and NAACP protestors were packed into filthy cells with no word of when, or *if*, they would be released. Protest leaders called King, asking him to come and help them. King had been enjoying some time at home with his newborn son, Dexter, the Kings' third child, but King sensed that what was happening in southern Georgia was important. The very next morning, King and Abernathy flew to Albany.

At first, King was impressed by the spirit of blacks in Albany. As he spoke to large crowds, they seemed fired up and ready to follow the same path that blacks in Montgomery had followed during the bus boycott. But that was not to be. Blacks were reluctant to take action when the time came to boycott the bus system. And, because the black population was small in Albany, those who *did* boycott stores and buses didn't have much of an impact. Worse still, some blacks were willing to work with racists to stop the protests if they could get paid for it.

Perhaps most frustrating to King was the behavior of Albany's police chief, Laurie Pritchett. Pritchett was well aware that meeting the protestors' nonviolence with clubs and tear gas would only draw worldwide attention to Albany. Pritchett had watched his television closely and had noticed how the coverage of bombings in Birmingham and the beatings of Freedom Riders throughout the South had helped the civil rights movement. Pritchett had even studied Gandhi so that he would know what King's next moves might be.

As a result, King and the protestors could not get Pritchett and his officers to react with anger. The press then began to lose interest. Perhaps protestors were being jailed, but that wasn't "exciting" enough to put on the nightly news. When King was jailed, he was actually relieved. He was certain that this would bring the spotlight to Albany, and he was determined to stay in jail as long as it would take. However, when King was told that the city had agreed to the demands of the protestors, he posted bail so that he could celebrate the victory with the black residents of Albany.

But there was no victory. The police officers had lied to King in order to trick him into posting bail. King was ashamed and angry to have paid his way out of jail for no reason.

Segregation remained as strong as ever in Albany, Georgia. The press began to leave, dismissing the Albany movement as a failure. What they never caught on film, however, was the police officers' violence, which was kept carefully hidden from the cameras. One night, a pregnant woman, who was taking food to some of the jailed protestors, was severely beaten by officers in a dark alley behind the jail. Later that night, when word of the beating spread through the black community, tempers flared. Blacks stormed downtown and rioted, throwing bottles and rocks at policemen.

"Look at that nonviolence!" Pritchett said with a big grin to the handful of newspeople who came out to cover the riot. He carefully pointed out how the blacks were being violent, while his officers remained peaceful. Some of the newspeople shook their heads and laughed along. Pritchett was right. Was the "peaceful" civil rights movement falling apart?

Albany was a huge blow to King and his push for a nonviolent movement. Days later, he and Abernathy left Albany, feeling that all their work there had been in vain. Looking back on what had happened in Albany, King realized that trying to desegregate *everything* had been too much. The focus should have been on one or two things—lunch counters or buses or parks. But trying to end segregation entirely had been too much.

"Our protest was so vague that we got nothing," King wrote, "and the people were left very depressed and in despair."

We've come too far to turn back!

King remembered the words he had spoken to the 1,200 protestors the night they were trapped and frightened in the Montgomery First Baptist Church. He knew there was no choice but to learn from the mistakes made in Albany and move on. It was time to find the right place and the right issue to launch another demonstration, a *successful* demonstration. Little did King know that one of the biggest demonstrations of the civil rights movement was about to begin.

CHAPTER 8

As Martin Luther King, Jr., and other leaders met in the fall of 1962 to put together their next plan of action, a young black man named James Meredith walked onto the campus of the University of Mississippi. Immediately, he was surrounded by a crowd of club-wielding police officers and a scowling lieutenant governor of Mississippi. He was told to get off the campus.

Although Meredith had the legal right to attend the university, neither the people of Mississippi nor the governor, Ross Barnett, would stand for it. The governor didn't care about the law or the fact that even President Kennedy had told him that he must let Meredith on campus. He said that "Ole Miss," as the school was called, would not be desegregated.

"The Negro is different, because God made him different to punish him," the governor was known to say fairly often. And when it came to blacks attending Ole Miss, the school he himself had attended, Barnett actually suggested that it would be deadly to the white race to allow blacks to live among them.

"There is no case in history where the Caucasian race has survived social integration," he barked on television the evening of September 13. With that, he ordered state officials to go to jail rather than obey the court orders to allow Meredith to attend Ole Miss.

What followed was the most brutal and deadly conflict between the federal government and a state government since the Civil War.

On the evening of September 30, 1962, President Kennedy ordered 300 federal marshals to surround Ole Miss. James Meredith was scheduled to enter the campus that evening, and the President wanted him to be protected. Meanwhile, hundreds of angry, shouting, Confederate-flag-waving racists gathered near the campus gates. They broke bottles and waved guns at the marshals.

When the marshals tossed tear gas into the mob to get the crowd to break up, the people responded with gunfire. What took place throughout the night was no less than warfare. When morning finally came, two men had been killed, and hundreds, both marshals and members of the angry mob, had been injured.

Kennedy was furious. Throughout the next month, more than 20,000 troops were put in place to keep peace at Ole Miss and protect Meredith, who finally entered the campus and began classes. The battle for desegregation at Ole Miss had been won, but at what cost? People had been killed and wounded. And Meredith spent two years at a school where not one other student would talk to him or even sit near him. It was a bitter victory indeed.

King watched the James Meredith story with sadness. There was so much violence over just one black man entering an all-white college. If nothing else, it proved, yet again, how much hard work there was still to do in the South. King thought about how Ole Miss had long been considered the most fiercely segregated university in the United States. Yet Meredith had specifically chosen it as the school he would attend.

Meredith's choice made King think. It occurred to him that the civil rights movement would gain the most ground and the most attention by focusing on changing things in the most segregated city imaginable. Then King knew without a doubt where the next civil rights campaign must take place: Birmingham, Alabama.

"In the entire country, there was no place to compare with Birmingham," King would later write. "It was a community in which human rights had been trampled on for so long that fear and oppression were as thick in its atmosphere as the smog from its factories."

Early in 1963, King and Abernathy and other SCLC leaders met to plan what they would focus on in Birmingham. They decided to begin by protesting the segregation at lunch counters, restrooms, and water fountains. They would use both sit-ins and peaceful demonstrations, such as marches and mass prayer. King and the other members of the Southern Christian Leadership Conference knew they would be in for a battle. George Wallace, the governor of Alabama, had used "Segregation Forever!" as his campaign slogan in 1962.

In addition, Birmingham's commissioner of public safety, Eugene "Bull" Connor, was a stubborn and angry racist. He was the man who had "allowed" the Klan to attack the Freedom Riders for fifteen minutes. Bull Connor was so unconcerned with the safety of blacks in Birmingham that when black people were murdered, their killers were rarely sentenced or even tried. Bombings of black homes and churches went uninvestigated, and there were so many bombings that Birmingham was often referred to as "Bombingham."

In the midst of all the planning and worry about Birmingham, the Kings' fourth child, Bernice, was born. King was a devoted father who loved nothing more than playing with his children on the swing set in the backyard or, sometimes to Coretta's annoyance, chasing them wildly all over the house as they whooped with laughter. On the rare evenings when King was home, the children would gather around him at bedtime and listen to him read their favorite stories.

King wanted to see racism and segregation change so that his children would have better lives. In many of King's speeches, he talked about a painful incident involving his oldest child. When Yolanda was six years old, she had seen a commercial about a new amusement park in Atlanta called "Funtown." She asked her father again and again if he would take her to the park, but King always had a different excuse for not taking her. Finally, with tears in her eyes, Yolanda looked at her father and said, "You just don't want to take me."

Although Yolanda was just a young child, King had to explain a very difficult thing to her: Funtown was for white people only. Black children were not allowed to go there. King could tell by his daughter's confused and hurt expression that this was the first time she had realized that the mere color of her skin set her apart and made some people dislike her. As Yolanda's tears fell, her father could barely contain his own.

So it was with both personal sorrow and an ongoing sorrow for his entire race that King headed to Birmingham to fight against the most bitter segregation in the United States.

In April of 1963, "Project C" began. "Project C" was the name that King and the SCLC had given to the movement in Birmingham. The "C" stood for "confrontation," but Bull Connor did not know that. As before, the confrontation by black protestors would be peaceful, but firm. If the city would not give in to the demands to desegregate facilities, the protests would become larger and more determined.

King encouraged blacks to meet nightly at a Birmingham church so that they could learn how to protest peacefully. King named the thousands of blacks who became trained in this kind of protest the "nonviolent army." These men and women would serve in what would become known as the "battle in Birmingham." King and other leaders encouraged the protestors to march, sing hymns, even kneel and pray in the middle of the street to block traffic, but they were not to raise their voices or fists in anger.

Bull Connor, like Laurie Pritchett in Albany, knew that use of violence would bring in swarms of television crews and would increase sympathy for the civil rights movement. So, in the beginning, he warned police officers to use arrest as the only response to protests. However, King knew Bull Connor's reputation well. Connor was very short-tempered, and he had already angrily announced that he was not about to let "a bunch of niggers" take control of Birmingham. King knew it was just a matter of time before Bull Connor's short fuse would burn down.

At first, Connor simply and quietly filled the jails with marchers who would not leave the crowd and go home. He charged them with disturbing the peace. Then Connor managed to get a court order that called for the demonstrations to end. Now, it would be illegal, not just a disturbance, for blacks to march. King had never intentionally broken the law before, but now he felt that he and the demonstrators had no choice.

"It's better to go to jail with dignity," King thundered to the crowds gathered at the church that night, "than accept segregation in humility."

Bull Connor, as expected, grew angry. He hadn't expected King to willingly break the law and encourage his followers to do the same. He had fully expected King to be afraid and back down.

"You can rest assured," Connor snarled back in response, "that I will fill the jails if these Negroes violate the laws."

The next morning, Good Friday, King and Abernathy met the protestors at the church and reminded them to remain calm as they were arrested. For his part, King announced, "I am prepared to go to jail and stay as long as necessary." He would not be tricked or pressured into paying bail this time around. With that, King and Abernathy led the protestors down Main Street and toward City Hall, all of them singing "We Shall Overcome."

Immediately, Bull Connor and his police came charging toward the nonviolent army. Conner, red-faced, screamed to his policemen to arrest every one of the protestors. King and Abernathy fell to their knees in front of Connor and began to pray quietly. Furious, Connor ordered King to be thrown into solitary confinement. This would be the thirteenth time King had been arrested during his years of civil rights work, but he had never before been in solitary.

"You will never know the meaning of utter darkness," King would later write of his solitary confinement, "until you have lain in such a dungeon, knowing that sunlight is streaming overhead and still seeing only darkness below."

King's cell was a filthy, dark hole with no mattress or pillow. No one, not even his lawyers or family, was allowed to see King. Friday became Saturday in a long blur of darkness broken up only by occasional plates of disgusting food being shoved through the small cell doorway. King fell into despair as the hours of Easter Sunday dragged on. But his sorrow was for others, not himself. How worried was Coretta? How disappointed were his children without their father home on one of their favorite holidays? And what was happening with the movement in Birmingham? King feared that with so many protestors and leaders in jail, the movement could be falling apart.

Finally, relief came on Monday morning. King received a mattress and blankets, and he was allowed to call Coretta. Coretta told King that when President Kennedy had heard about his imprisonment, he had called the Birmingham jail directly to ask how King was being treated.

After that call, King's jailers allowed King to have visitors and read the local newspapers. King was happy to find out that the protests in Birmingham were still taking place, but another article in the paper upset him greatly.

A group of eight ministers, all white and of all different faiths, had written an article condemning the Birmingham movement. They referred to what King was doing as "extremist," and they called all who joined him "lawbreakers" and worse. However, what bothered King most was the clergymen's claim that what King was doing was "untimely." The ministers thought that those involved in the civil rights movement were being too impatient. They felt that black people should just be quiet and wait.

Wait. The word was too much for King to bear.

He had no paper to write on, but Martin Luther King, Jr., began a letter in response to the clergymen. He wrote in the margins of many newspaper pages and even on paper napkins. King's 6,500-word reply would come to be honored as one of the most important and moving documents in American history: "Letter from Birmingham Jail."

"Perhaps it is easy for those who have never felt the stinging darts of segregation to say, 'Wait,'" King wrote. "But when you have seen vicious mobs lynch your mothers and fathers at will and drown your sisters and brothers at whim; when you have seen hate-filled policemen curse, kick and even kill your black brothers and sisters; when you see the vast majority of your twenty million Negro brothers smothering in an airtight cage of poverty . . . when you are forever fighting a degenerating sense of 'nobodiness'—then you will understand why we find it difficult to wait."

When King was released from jail, eight days after his arrest, he was disappointed to see that the battle in Birmingham had come to a halt. Most of the original protestors had also just gotten out of jail, and they were in no hurry to get thrown back in. As a result, one of King's aides came up with an unusual plan. Many young people, even children, had been eager to march in the protests. Why not let the children become the new "nonviolent army"?

At first, King said no. He feared for the safety of the children if Bull Connor finally lost his temper completely. Still, King continued thinking about it. These were children who lived with the threat of bombings, bullying, and humiliation every day. These were young people whose self-esteem would be slowly destroyed if Jim Crow laws remained in effect in Birmingham. Could the anger of Bull Connor be worse than that? Finally, King agreed to let the children march. What began on May 2, 1963, would become known as "The Children's Crusade."

More than 1,000 young people, many of them between the ages of six and seventeen, marched through downtown Birmingham on May 2. Many were arrested, but that didn't dampen the children's spirits. The next day, 2,500 young people marched. As they moved through the streets, they chanted, "We Want Freedom!" and sang hymns and freedom songs. Bull Connor was frustrated that the children had returned in bigger numbers. He ordered them to stop and go home. When they ignored him and continued marching and chanting, Connor reached his breaking point.

"Let 'em have it!" he screamed to the surrounding police officers and firemen.

Police released German shepherds that lunged at the terrified children, biting and tearing the clothes off many of them. Some of the younger children panicked and turned to run toward the adults and parents who had been watching the march.

"Look at 'em run!" Connor laughed, pointing at the children. "Look at those little niggers run!"

But for every child who turned to run, many more stood their ground and turned the other cheek as they had been trained to do. Bravely, they continued marching and singing. Now Bull Connor was truly infuriated. He ordered firemen to turn on their powerful hoses and aim them at the children. The terrible force of the water threw children to the ground and slammed them against the sides of buildings.

Still, the children refused to give up. Many of them were bleeding and soaking wet, but they continued down the street, praying and singing. Connor, at his wit's end, sent in wave after wave of police officers to arrest every single child. Before the day ended, nearly 1,000 minors had been arrested and tossed into the city jails.

The next day, much to Bull Connor's rage, another 1,000 young people, led by adults this time, began walking toward the same downtown area. When they reached the police barricade, the adults motioned to the children, and the entire group fell to their knees and began praying.

"Turn on the hoses!" Connor shouted to the line of firemen as he pointed at the kneeling protestors.

Then, something totally unexpected happened. The firemen stood motionless, the hoses sagging in their hands. Several of the firemen fought back tears as they witnessed the remarkable courage and strength of the protestors—some as young as six years old.

"I said turn on the hoses, damn it!" Connor bellowed.

But as the protestors slowly rose to their feet, the firemen with their hoses and the policemen with their dogs all stood still. And as the protestors began moving down the street again, the officers parted for them and let them march on. Some of the officers bowed their heads and wiped their eyes—*all* of the officers deliberately refused to follow the orders being shouted by Bull Connor.

As Gandhi had taught and as King had believed, those in power were ultimately shamed into doing the right thing.

Later, Coretta Scott King would say of that moment, "It was the first crack in the morale of the racist forces."

CHAPTER 9

"The civil rights movement owes Bull Connor as much as it owes Abraham Lincoln," President Kennedy said wryly as the protests continued in Birmingham.

And it was true. As King had suspected all along, Connor was not able to control his temper, and when he lost it, the entire world watched. When Connor had barked out orders to attack children with dogs and fire hoses, and had given the go-ahead to hit women with clubs, the media swarmed to get film, pictures, and interviews. Understandably, people everywhere were horrified by the ugly images of hate. Up to this point, no other event in the entire movement had gained so much sympathy and support from the watching world.

"To people everywhere," Coretta would

later write, "Bull Connor came to represent the force of evil."

Even though many of the white residents of Birmingham were among those appalled by Connor's behavior, the city leaders continued to drag their feet on the issues of desegregation. Finally, President Kennedy sent an attorney from Washington, D.C., to Birmingham to try to work out an agreement. Still, the city hesitated. In a final demonstration of unity, many thousands of black protestors from all over Alabama packed the streets of downtown Birmingham.

"There were square blocks of Negroes," King wrote, "a veritable sea of black faces. They were committing no violence; they were just present and singing."

They may have been just "present and singing," but many of the downtown business owners had had enough. They began pressuring the city to agree to the changes that the demonstrators wanted. Finally, on May 10, 1963, Birmingham officials agreed to *all* of the demands that King and the other SCLC leaders had requested two months earlier. It was a major victory.

However, as it had been in Montgomery after the bus boycott victory, so it was in Birmingham—racist anger exploded. King had returned to Atlanta, but a phone call from his brother, A.D., who lived in Birmingham, woke him in the middle of the night. A.D.'s home had been bombed twice by the Ku Klux Klan. Immediately after the Klan had destroyed A.D.'s home, they bombed the hotel where King had been staying, hoping that he might still be in his room.

The timing of the bombings had been intentional. It was a Saturday night, and in the black neighborhoods where the bombs had been placed, the bars and clubs were full. Blacks poured out of the clubs and began rioting, giving Alabama's racist governor, Wallace, all the reason he needed to send in the National Guard. Although the Klan had started all the trouble, blacks were punished. Black neighborhoods were sealed off by Guardsmen who threatened anyone seen loitering or, sometimes, simply walking along the sidewalk.

This led to even more rioting. King and Abernathy rushed back to Birmingham and traveled through the black neighborhoods, pleading with residents to remain calm. They even walked into the rougher bars and poolrooms to preach their message of nonviolence. Many of the men in those bars were so moved by King's words that they handed over guns and knives to King and Abernathy to prove that they would not use violence to express their anger.

Just as tempers in Birmingham seemed to be settling down, Governor Wallace pulled national attention back to Alabama.

"Segregation now, segregation tomorrow, and segregation forever!" had been Wallace's theme during his run for governor, and it remained his theme even after the agreement in Birmingham. Wallace had often stated that he personally would block the door of any all-white public school in Alabama if black students tried to enter.

And on June 11, 1963, Wallace did just that. As two black students attempted to enter a building at the University of Alabama, Wallace folded his arms and blocked their way, refusing to move from the doorway. Although it was now against federal law to keep black students out of white schools, Wallace didn't care. He told the press that he'd have to be picked up and carried away before he'd move.

President Kennedy, who had remained somewhat reluctant to become directly involved in the civil rights movement, now took action. He called in the National Guard to escort the black students onto the campus, and he personally ordered Wallace to remove himself from the doorway.

More important, Kennedy went on live national television and delivered a stirring and supportive speech about the civil rights movement. It was the first time a United States President had ever done this.

"Like our soldiers and sailors in all parts of the world," Kennedy said of blacks involved in civil rights protests, "they are meeting freedom's challenge on the firing line, and I salute them for their honor and their courage."

As to keeping black young people out of white schools, Kennedy said, "This is one country. It has become one country because all of us and all the people who came here had an equal chance to develop their talents. We cannot say to ten percent of the population that you can't have that right."

It was a speech that inspired a nation. Both black and white people now wanted to be part of this important movement, and the slogan "Free in '63" swept the nation. It was chanted in marches and even in churches. In small towns throughout the South and in big cities in the North, blacks had watched the speech, cheering and crying.

And in the small town of Jackson, Mississippi, a young man named Medgar Evers happily heaved a deep sigh of relief to hear the nation's leader declare that blacks could not and would not be denied entrance to any school in the land.

He had recently watched the riots and death that accompanied James Meredith's entrance into the segregated University of Mississippi. Meredith was the first black to get into this school—although it required the full force of the United States government.

Eight years before, in 1954, Evers had tried to enroll in the University of Mississippi's law school. His application had been instantly rejected with no explanation.

Evers had then dedicated his life to fighting segregation. For ten years, he had organized meetings, worked with the NAACP, and led demonstrations. Like King, he often received death threats, but they didn't frighten Evers.

"I love my children, and I love my wife with all my heart," Evers often said. "And I would die, and die gladly, if that would make a better life for them."

On the night of Kennedy's speech, Evers returned home around midnight. Wearing a t-shirt that said "Jim Crow Must Go," Evers got out of his car and walked toward his house. Suddenly, a gunshot echoed in the night. Evers had been shot in the back at close range. Inside the house, his young son heard the noise and ran out to find his father sprawled across the ground. Medgar Evers reached toward his son and whispered, "Help me, my son, help me." But before the boy could even reach his father, Evers died. The force of the bullet had been so strong that it had passed through Evers, entered the house, broken through the living room wall, flown into the kitchen, and dented the refrigerator.

People everywhere were outraged and saddened to hear about the brutal murder of Medgar Evers. That it took place on the same night as Kennedy's speech was almost too much to bear. However, this untimely death further fanned the flames of the civil rights movement and motivated thousands of additional people to get involved and demand equality.

"This tragic occurrence," King said the next day, "should cause all persons . . . to be more determined than ever before to break down all the barriers of racial segregation and discrimination."

Evers was not the first person to give his life for the civil rights movement, and he would not be the last. But if he had hoped that his own death might help the movement proceed, his hopes were fulfilled.

"You can kill a man," Evers had said not long before his own death, "but you can't kill an idea."

President Kennedy, in his historic speech, had discussed the creation of a civil rights bill. This would be a piece of legislation that would make all forms of segregation and discrimination illegal throughout the United States. However, Kennedy had not been specific about when this bill would be designed or passed.

King and other civil rights leaders worried. Kennedy had been slow and reluctant to act before. Would he simply set the idea of a civil rights bill aside and forget about it? 1963 had been a tremendous year for the movement, and it was barely half over. With such momentum, many felt that the time to pass a civil rights bill was *now*. The time of waiting was over.

Along with other leaders, King agreed that some sort of major statement needed to be made, some kind of event that would draw the attention of the world—and particularly the President. The leaders thought the best idea was to have a mass gathering in Washington, D.C., right in Kennedy's view. The gathering would have two purposes: to honor the memory of Medgar Evers and to show support for a civil rights bill.

Called the "March on Washington for Jobs and Freedom," the gathering was set for August 28, 1963. It would be a simple march in the National Mall from the Washington Monument to the Lincoln Memorial (less than a mile) and then an afternoon of entertainment and speeches. Entertainers included Sidney Poitier, Joan Baez, Bob Dylan, Harry Belafonte, and Mahalia Jackson. Organizers hoped that the big names would draw 100,000 people or more.

President Kennedy was not enthusiastic about a mass march on the nation's capital. He felt that a private meeting with civil rights leaders would be more dignified and more likely to lead to Congress passing a civil rights bill.

"We want success in Congress," Kennedy told King, "not just a big show at the Capitol."

King politely disagreed. He and other leaders did not think of the march as a "big show." They hoped that the sight of many thousands gathered, all in support of one idea, would not only lead Congress to make the right decision, but also lead people worldwide to make their own personal decision to support human rights.

The night before the march, King worked

feverishly on his speech. It was to be a fairly short speech, but King wanted every word to count. This was, after all, the most important speech he had ever given. When Coretta woke at dawn in the hotel where she and Martin were staying, she heard her husband's typewriter—he was just finishing his speech, exhausted but happy with what he had written. Still, King worried whether his carefully chosen words would inspire the crowd. He wanted his speech to be more than just a "good speech." He wanted it to touch the hearts of those gathered.

As King and his wife prepared to head over to the Mall, they listened to news reports with disappointment. "A very small crowd has gathered," the reporters continued to say, "possibly fewer than 25,000 people."

However, when Martin and Coretta reached the Mall, it was quite a different story.

"By the time we arrived," Coretta would recall, "that whole vast, green concourse was alive with 250,000 people. . . . and almost a fourth of that enormous crowd was white. It was a beautiful sight."

It was the largest crowd ever gathered in Washington, D.C. People of every race had traveled from all over the United States to show their strong support for both the civil rights movement and the civil rights bill that Kennedy had spoken about. King was scheduled as the final speaker of the day, and when his name was announced, the crowd began chanting his name in a rhythmic way: "Martin Luther King! Martin Luther King!"

King stared out across the vast sea of people with pride, awe, and gratitude. As the cheering died down, he began his speech, quietly at first, and then his voice rose into the emotional thunder that he had become so well known for. Suddenly, something unexpected and wonderful happened.

King paused and looked at the faces of so many people who had bravely fought against discrimination. Some of them had gone to jail, some of them had been beaten, and some of them knew someone who had been killed. King sensed that these people needed something more, something *deeper* than the formal speech he had prepared. At that very moment, King turned away from the words he had spent all night carefully putting together, and he began to speak from his heart.

Coretta, who was sitting near her husband, remembered it well. "It seemed to all of us there that day that his words flowed from some higher place, through Martin, to the weary people before him. Heaven itself opened up, and we all seemed transformed."

The words King spoke from that point on would become known as his legendary "I Have a Dream" speech.

"I have a dream that one day on the red hills of Georgia, the sons of former slaves and the sons of former slave owners will be able to sit down together at the table of brotherhood.

"I have a dream that one day even the state of Mississippi, a state sweltering with the heat of injustice, sweltering with the heat of oppression, will be transformed into an oasis of freedom and justice.

"I have a dream that my four little children will one day live in a nation where they will not be judged by the color of their skin but by the content of their character.

"I have a *dream* today!"

When King finished, his hands raised to the heavens, the crowd of 250,000 seemed momentarily stunned. Then followed wave after wave of cheering, of stomping feet, and frenzied clapping. King was so overcome with emotion that he had to be helped back to his seat.

Kennedy, who had been watching television coverage of the march, was quite impressed. He and Vice President Lyndon Johnson invited all of the speakers and leaders to the White House for a reception. When Kennedy went around shaking every man's hand, he stopped at King and smiled at him.

"*I* have a dream," Kennedy said warmly.

King was embarrassed to have been singled out for the President's admiration. After all, many wonderful and powerful speeches had been delivered on that historic afternoon. Still, King was encouraged by Kennedy's response. It had been quite a day indeed.

"As television beamed the image of this extraordinary gathering across the border oceans," King would later write, "everyone who believed in man's capacity to better himself had a moment of inspiration and confidence in the future of the human race."

However, barely two weeks later, a horrific event would, yet again, test King's confidence in the human race.

CHAPTER 10

In the hours just before sunrise, on a warm Sunday morning in September of 1963, four men crept quietly around the Sixteenth Street Baptist Church in Birmingham, Alabama. One of the men crawled beneath some stairs and through a passageway that led to the basement of the church. In his arms, he carried 122 sticks of dynamite and a time-release instrument. After carefully placing the dynamite near a room where he thought churchgoers would be gathering, he set the timer for mid-morning and crawled back out to meet his friends. Grinning, the four Ku Klux Klan members congratulated one another and sneaked back to their car.

At 10:22 a.m. a group of black children began walking to a basement room to finish their prayers after listening to a sermon titled "The Love That Forgives." Suddenly, a sound like distant thunder rumbled, shaking the walls. Then a terrific blast shattered windows and threw screaming children to the ground. It was an explosion so severe that the entire back of the church was destroyed, cars on the street were damaged, and all but one stained-glass window in the church was blown out. The sole remaining window pictured Jesus Christ knocking on a door.

The walls, cars, and windows could be replaced. What could never be replaced were the lives of four young girls. Addie Collins, Denise McNair, Carole Robertson, and Cynthia Wesley were all killed instantly when the dynamite exploded. It was a crime so senseless and so hateful that it led King to despair.

"The children were the victims of a brutality which echoed around the world," King wrote. "Where was God in the midst of falling bombs?"

Adding to the pain was the indifference of Birmingham whites. Not much attention was paid to the horrific crime, and though one of the four men was accused of placing the dynamite in the church, he would not be convicted and put in prison for many years. The others who had worked with him would not go to prison until 2001 and 2002, nearly forty years later.

"These were friends of mine," a woman

interviewed in 2003 said of the four girls. "And we come to Sunday school one day, and they're gone. They're dead. They're just blown away, and Birmingham goes on with business as usual."

But the girls did not die in vain. Many consider the Sixteenth Street Church bombing to be a turning point in the civil rights movement. People, both black and white, who had stood on the sidelines watching and wondering if they should get involved, were so angered and saddened by the deaths of the four girls that they rushed to support the fight for civil rights.

On the other hand, as support grew, some black people, particularly in Birmingham, began questioning whether the peaceful resistance that King supported was worth the patience and sacrifice. Some felt that refusing to strike back in anger only encouraged racists to keep using violence.

"Negroes must now be prepared to protect themselves with guns," one black writer said, claiming that the days of nonviolence had come to an abrupt end on that September morning.

King hurried to Birmingham to help calm the tension and anger. He had heard rumblings about the need for blacks to use violence well before the church bombing, and now he knew that people were on the verge of throwing away years of peaceful protest in favor of an eye for an eye. King spoke at the funeral services for the four girls: "God still has a way of wringing good out evil," King assured the mourners as he encouraged blacks to continue on the path of peace.

In Washington, President Kennedy was now determined to draw up a civil rights bill. Between the massive and multiracial show of support at the March on Washington and the horror of the church bombing, he knew the time had come for some serious legislation. He invited King and other black leaders to come to Washington for a meeting. Together, they drew up a bill that would become the Civil Rights Act. Like all bills, it would have to pass the Senate and the House of Representatives before becoming a law, but everything looked promising. King returned home to Atlanta full of optimism. It seemed that change was right around the corner.

However, the change around the corner was not good.

"John Fitzgerald Kennedy, the 35th President of the United States, is dead at the age of 46," a radio announcer's shaky voice informed listeners on November 22, 1963.

"Shot by an assassin as he drove through the streets of Dallas, Texas, less than an hour ago. . . . the President is dead, killed in Dallas, Texas, by a gunshot wound."

In the King household, everyone was stunned—even eight-year-old Yolanda.

"Mommy! Mommy!" Yolanda shouted as she ran in the door from school. "They've killed President Kennedy, and he didn't do one single thing to anybody. We're never going to get our freedom now!" Yolanda concluded in tears.

To King, the loss of a man who was not only a great leader but also a personal friend was crushing. King was so emotionally overwhelmed that for three days he lay sick in bed. In the back of his mind, King, like his young daughter, did consider that the Civil Rights Act might now be pushed aside, but that worry was secondary to his concern for his country. King worried that hate and violence in the United States was like a contagious and deadly disease. And now it was spreading.

The evening after Kennedy was killed, Martin and Coretta sat quietly together. Then King looked directly at his wife and said, "This is what is going to happen to me also. I keep telling you, this is a sick society."

Another moment of silence passed as Coretta simply grasped King's hand in hers.

"I don't think I'm going to live to reach forty," King finally said in a hushed voice.

King need not have worried about the future of the Civil Rights Act. Only five days after Kennedy was killed, the new President, Lyndon B. Johnson, spoke to the members of Congress.

"No memorial oration or eulogy could more eloquently honor President Kennedy's memory than the earliest possible passage of the civil rights bill for which he fought so long," Johnson said.

Johnson was a Southerner, but, like growing numbers of white Southerners, he strongly supported equality for black people. Still, many Southerners warned Johnson that he was ruining his political career by supporting the civil rights bill. Johnson ignored the warnings. He worked extremely hard to get both the House of Representatives and the Senate to pass the bill. And while the Senate delayed the bill longer than it had delayed any other bill in Senate history, the civil rights bill was finally passed on July 2, 1964.

Along with many other leaders, King attended the signing of the Civil Rights Act in the East Room of the White House. King watched over Johnson's shoulder with a broad smile on his face. Finally, all segregation, Jim

Crow laws, and discrimination based on race would be illegal throughout the United States. When Johnson was finished signing, he turned around to shake King's hand first. Then, with a grin, Johnson handed King the pen he had used. King would keep it forever as a memento of that wonderful day.

King was remembered to have said that the Civil Rights Act, while physically written by the President and other leaders, was more truly "written in the streets" by the millions of brave protestors who had stood for what they knew was right and fair.

However, as King knew all too well, changing the law does nothing to change hatred and anger. And during the summer of 1964, this was proven again and again.

In June, three civil rights workers, James Chaney, Michael Schwerner, and Andrew Goodman, were driving to a small town in Mississippi to investigate a church bombing. Schwerner and Goodman were white men from New York, and Chaney was a black man from Mississippi. Suddenly, police lights flooded their car, and the three men pulled over. The police officer charged them with speeding—but they may not have been speeding at all. The officer, like a number of police officers in small Southern towns, was a member of the Ku Klux Klan, and he had been tipped off that these three activists might be headed his way. Instead of writing a ticket, the officer threw them all into jail.

Much later, in the darkest part of the night, the three men were released. They were denied phone calls. They were simply told to get out of town—quickly. As the men drove down a deserted back road looking for the highway, police lights chased them down again. It was the same officer, but this time he just told them to stay in their car and wait. In minutes, two truckloads of Ku Klux Klansmen arrived. The two white men were dragged out and shot in the head. The black man was beaten with chains, stabbed repeatedly, and finally shot.

Law officials in the small town shrugged their shoulders when the media grilled them with questions about what had happened to the three civil rights workers. The local sheriff just shook his head and said, "They're probably just hiding and trying to cause a lot of bad publicity for this part of the state." And Mississippi's governor laughed out loud and said, "They could be in Cuba."

Soon it became the focus of the entire country, and search crews, the FBI, and CIA investigators descended upon the town. Six weeks later the men's car was finally found burned and buried in a secluded swamp. The bodies of the men were dug up not far from their car. Many years later, the Klansmen involved in the murders would finally be charged, but none would serve more than six years in prison.

Meanwhile, tempers of black people flared, and riots erupted in New York, New Jersey, Illinois, and Pennsylvania. In Northern cities, a majority of black people were poor and lived in slums. While white Northerners were generally open-minded about civil rights, they often ignored the conditions blacks lived in. Furthermore, whites frequently paid no attention to the rough way that policemen treated poor blacks, and this brutality set off many of the riots in Northern cities.

In Philadelphia in August of 1964, police arrested a young black woman when she became angry after being told to move her stalled car. Although the interaction was harmless enough, it drew a crowd in the black neighborhood. Tension had been mounting for several years over how unfairly and cruelly police treated the black residents of Philadelphia. Now, people could control their tempers no longer. One man attacked the arresting officer, while others began breaking windows of white-owned businesses. Rioting continued for three very hot days. By the time it was all over, 341 people were injured, 774 people were arrested, and 225 stores were damaged or destroyed.

King followed all of this with dismay. There was a growing feeling among many young blacks that King and the SCLC were old-fashioned and out of touch with what was happening. These young people, many of them high school and college students, had watched blacks continue to get discriminated against, beaten, and even killed. They'd had enough. They believed it was time to strike back in righteous anger. Now, when King traveled to Northern cities to preach nonviolence, he was occasionally booed.

Fueling this new move toward violence were the fiery speeches of the radical leader Malcolm X. Malcolm felt that King had spent too much time trying to work alongside white people. To Malcolm, white people were a dangerous enemy that could never be trusted. Malcolm looked at King's approach as being too polite, too slow—even cowardly. Malcolm X wanted a revolution, not a peaceful march.

"Who ever heard of angry revolutionists all harmonizing 'We Shall Overcome Some Day' while tripping and swaying along arm-in-arm with the very people they were supposed to be angrily revolting against?" Malcolm X thundered to crowds of young blacks. "Who ever heard of angry revolutionists swinging their bare feet together with their oppressor in lily-pad park pools, with gospels and guitars and 'I Have a Dream' speeches? And meanwhile the black masses in America were—and still are— having a nightmare."

Obviously, Martin Luther King, Jr., and Malcolm X did not agree with one another on which approach to take to gain civil rights. Still, both men admired one another for their intelligence and their passion. King felt that Malcolm's anger resulted from the violence and poverty he had grown up in.

"He, like so many of our number, was a victim of despair," King would later write. And when, in 1965, Malcolm X was murdered, King mourned the loss. The two had not seen eye to eye, but they had shared the same vision: a day when all black people in America would be treated fairly.

Near the end of 1964, King was very tired. He had had a busy year of traveling across the country and back, making speeches in support of nonviolence in an increasingly violent time. Sometimes King wondered if the era of peaceful protest was slowly slipping away. In big cities in both the North and the West, the patience of blacks who felt ignored and brushed aside was nearly gone. Reports of fierce rioting became more and more common on the evening news.

On one weekend in October, King had given four speeches in the Northeast, and had then flown to St. Louis to deliver three more speeches on Monday. Tuesday morning, he flew back to Atlanta and was admitted to the hospital for exhaustion. He slept nearly twenty hours before the phone by his bed woke him up.

"Martin! Martin!" Coretta's excited voice came through the receiver. "You've won the Nobel Peace Prize!"

King sat up and stared into space. Was he still asleep and dreaming?

"What?" King asked, dazed.

"Martin, the committee has chosen you. You've won the Nobel Peace Prize," Coretta repeated.

King could hardly believe it. This was the biggest honor he had ever received. The Nobel Peace Prize was awarded each year to the one person in the *entire world* who had done the most to promote peace and harmony. At 35, King would be the youngest person ever to have received the award. He would be only the second African American to be honored in this way.

Suddenly, King was no longer tired. As calls poured in from friends, family, and even President Johnson, King's mind raced ahead. He and Coretta would need to get ready to go to Oslo, Norway, where all Nobel Prizes were awarded. And, once again, he would need to prepare just the right speech for the acceptance of this impressive award.

Later that fall, King stood in a room filled with important leaders from around the world as he was awarded the Peace Prize. The award itself consisted of a medal, a diploma, and a check. King smiled as he looked at the shiny gold medal with the words *Pro pace et fraternitate gentium* etched on it. Translated from Latin, this means "For the peace and brotherhood of men." King would treasure the medal, but he had already made up his mind to donate every penny of the $54,000 check to the civil rights movement.

It had been a very difficult year for peace in the United States. Still, in King's acceptance speech, he spoke of his continuing faith in the ways of nonviolent protest and in the ability to love one's enemies.

"I believe that unarmed truth and unconditional love will have the final word," King said that evening in Oslo. "I still believe that we shall overcome."

CHAPTER 11

On his way home from Oslo, Martin Luther King, Jr., stopped in Washington, D.C., to meet with President Johnson. King wanted to speak with the President about creating a voting rights bill for black Americans. Even though the Civil Rights Act made it illegal to discriminate against black people, in some parts of the South white people continued to find ways to make life difficult for blacks. In particular, some whites were especially worried about blacks gaining political power. Keeping black people "in their place" was important to racists. They believed that if they could keep blacks from voting, blacks would not be elected to public office—and whites' positions of power would be secure.

To make their plan work, racists continued to find all sorts of ways to keep blacks from registering to vote. Often, blacks were required to take unfairly difficult tests or to memorize lengthy sections of the state's constitution. Sometimes they were told lies about the voter registration process. But most often, blacks were threatened and intimidated. A black man or woman who refused to give up the battle to become registered might find his or her home bombed. In some small Southern towns, newspapers printed the names of black voters the day after they had registered. More often than not, these blacks would be fired from their jobs the following day.

Intimidation worked. Throughout the South, blacks were afraid to register to vote. In many small towns where the population was mostly black, whites still remained in power. This bothered King a lot. After all, what good was the Civil Rights Act if blacks continued to remain powerless?

Still, President Johnson denied King's request for a voting rights bill. Johnson thought that one civil rights bill was enough. He worried about angering Southern senators and congressmen whose votes he would need in order to pass other bills.

"I'm sorry, Martin," Johnson simply responded. "Nothing can be done."

Nothing can be done. King was not about

to believe that. Something could *always* be done—change was *always* possible.

"Selma, Alabama, was to 1965 what Birmingham was to 1963," King wrote. In Selma, there were 15,000 black residents who were old enough to vote, but only 350 were registered. King and Abernathy decided to focus on Selma in much the same way they had focused on Birmingham. Selma, like Birmingham, was known to be an extremely racist city. Many whites in Selma totally ignored the new Civil Rights Act, knowing that blacks were generally too afraid to demand their rights. And, like Birmingham's Bull Connor, Selma's Sheriff Jim Clark was a narrow-minded, short-tempered man. King knew that Clark's short fuse was likely to draw national attention to the voting rights protests.

On February 1, 1965, King stood before a crowd of 700 protestors near downtown Selma as they prepared to march to the city courthouse.

"Today is the day we will all go to jail!" King shouted to the crowd. Cheers erupted in response. King and those gathered knew that Jim Clark and his police force were waiting for them. There was no law against peaceful marching, but Clark, like Bull Connor, would invent some reason for arresting the protestors.

"Give us the ballot! Give us the ballot!" 700 voices thundered in unison as the group walked to the courthouse steps. Immediately, Clark's officers arrested everyone and crammed them into the small jail cells. Just as quickly, the press swarmed to Selma, eager to interview King.

"Why are we in jail?" King repeated when asked that question by a reporter. "Have you ever been required to answer one hundred questions on government . . . merely to vote? Have you ever stood in line with over a hundred others and, after an entire day, seen less than ten given the qualifying test? This is Selma, Alabama. There are more Negroes in jail with me than there are on the voting rolls."

As expected, it took little time for Sheriff Jim Clark to lose his temper. After King and the protestors were released, they gathered again the very next morning, chanting outside the courthouse. Clark was filmed hitting a female protestor and using cattle prods and bullwhips to push the marchers toward the jails. On his lapel, Clark proudly wore a button that read NEVER. *Never* would he allow equal rights for blacks in his city.

As King and the marchers were repeatedly jailed, blacks in surrounding towns began their own small protests. Generally, the protests were peaceful, but then tragedy struck in nearby Marion, Alabama. As protestors had marched to the town square, state troopers rushed in, trapping many of the marchers in a downtown restaurant. Officers then brutally swung their clubs at the trapped men and women. Twenty-five-year-old Jimmie Lee Jackson watched in horror as one of the officers raised his club high over his head, preparing to bring it down on Jimmie's mother, who cowered in a corner. Jimmie threw himself at the officer in an attempt to protect his mother, but the officer was faster. He shot Jimmie in the stomach. Jimmie managed to run out of the restaurant, but several officers chased him until he fell to the ground. Officers then surrounded Jimmie Lee Jackson, offering no assistance as he struggled in the dirt. Eight days later, Jackson died of an infected gunshot wound.

Back in Selma, the news of Jackson's death created fury. Some blacks vowed to hunt down the officers and kill them. Once again, King found himself, before a crowd of 2,000 people, pleading for a peaceful response to yet another brutal racist attack. Later that same day, one of King's associates, James Bevel, suggested a march to honor Jimmie Lee Jackson. The march would also protest police brutality.

King liked this idea, but protestors had marched so many times in Selma. How would this march be any different? Bevel had the answer. The march would only *begin* in Selma—then it would continue for fifty-four miles all the way to the state capitol in Montgomery. Protestors would be at the very door of Governor George Wallace's office. Wallace had long ignored civil rights activists in his state, but he would not be able to ignore them as they shouted from the steps of the Alabama capitol.

On March 7, 1965, 600 protestors gathered at a church in Selma. King was not able to be there for the start of the fifty-four-mile trek, but he assured the marchers that he would join them on Monday. In Montgomery, Wallace had received news of the march and was immediately angered by it. Without a second thought, he gave Sheriff Jim Clark permission to put an end to the marching.

"Use any means necessary," Wallace instructed. Clark gladly agreed to do just that. Now he had the legal right to be as violent as he wanted.

As the 600 marchers, led by John Lewis and Hosea Williams, crested the Edmund Pettus Bridge leading out of town, they faced a chilling sight. A solid wall of state troopers blocked the street. The troopers, led by Jim Clark, stood with clubs and whips ready. Some sat on horseback with rifles in their hands.

"Turn around and go back to your church!" an officer repeated through a bullhorn. "You have only two minutes to turn around. Two minutes! Go back now!"

But the marchers would not go back. With heads held high, the protestors walked silently and bravely, directly into the hornets' nest of troopers. What followed would become known as "Bloody Sunday." Clark gave a shout to attack, and the troopers fell upon the marchers, beating them with clubs and lashing them with heavy whips. The press filmed women being thrown to the ground and kicked, young people being cornered and gagged with tear gas, and white racists standing along the street cheering as though they were watching a sporting event.

When King watched the news that Sunday evening, he felt both angry and guilty. He hated to think that he had been safe in his own home while friends and supporters had been beaten bloody. King may have remembered words he had once spoken: "We begin to die inside the day we become silent about things that matter." There was only one thing to do.

"Not to try to march again would have been unthinkable," King wrote. In fewer than forty-eight hours, King stood with hundreds of marchers again in Selma.

"I say to you this afternoon," King shouted to the crowd, "that I would rather die on the highways of Alabama than make a butchery of my conscience. I say to you, when we march, don't panic and remember that we must remain true to nonviolence."

This time, as the marchers again faced the wall of police officers at the far side of the bridge, a U.S. marshal came forward and told King that a restraining order filed by a state judge made the march illegal. Thinking about this, King moved forward anyway. When he and the protestors reached the officers, they knelt and prayed. The officers, shamed by the gentle peacefulness of the crowd, stepped aside so that the marchers could continue. Sheriff Clark barked out orders for his officers to continue blocking the marchers' way, but his shouts were ignored.

However, King did not continue with the march that morning. He decided, instead, to fight against the restraining order over the next several days so that the protestors could march the fifty-four miles legally. So many of those marching had already spent days, even weeks, in jail. King felt it was only fair to let them march free from the worry of being imprisoned yet again.

Helping King with the details of fighting the order was a white minister from Boston named James Reeb. Reeb and King had been friends for several years, and both were glad they were working together in Selma. On March 9, after a long day of work, Reeb and two other white ministers decided to have dinner at a black-owned restaurant in Selma. White people never ate at black restaurants in Alabama in 1965, but Reeb and his friends were warmly welcomed—everyone knew who they were.

Unfortunately, racists knew who they were, too.

As Reeb and the two others left the restaurant, they were followed by a mob of white men carrying clubs and metal pipes. All three ministers were beaten unconscious and left for dead. Two of the ministers would survive the attack, but Reeb would not.

"This is an American tragedy," President Johnson announced on national television the day after Reeb died. That same day, Governor Wallace had flown to Washington to beg the President to force King and the protestors to cancel the march to Montgomery. Not only did Johnson deny Wallace's request, Johnson changed his mind about a voting rights bill. He now saw just how important it was to Americans—both black and white.

"Their cause must be our cause too," Johnson said in a speech to Congress. "Because it's not just Negroes, but really it's all of us who must overcome the crippling legacy of bigotry and injustice. And we *shall* overcome."

King, watching the speech with Abernathy and other leaders, smiled. And along with that smile, a tear rolled down his cheek.

More than 4,000 people gathered in Selma on March 21, 1965. The events, both tragic and wonderful, that surrounded the protests had attracted the attention of the world. Now people of all races and all backgrounds traveled to this small city in Alabama to be part of the historic fifty-four-mile march. Many would drop out along the way, but close to 25,000 people joined and rejoined near the end to walk the final six miles to the Alabama capitol.

Governor George Wallace sat in his office pouting angrily, his window shades drawn and his door locked. He could hear the singing and cheering outside, but he told his aides to tell the marchers that he was not in. Still, all day, and deep into the night, the many thousands outside listened to speeches and entertainers, and celebrated how far the civil rights movement had come. Rosa Parks, sitting up on the stage with King and others, smiled broadly.

"I looked at Rosa Parks," Coretta Scott King would later recall. "I sat there and began to think back over the years of struggle from 1955 to 1965. I realized we had really come a long way. . . ."

However, there was still a long way to go.

"As we entered the Watts area of Los Angeles," King wrote in late 1965, "all seemed quiet, but there could still be sensed raging hostility which had erupted in volcanic force in the days previous."

In August of 1965, Los Angeles experienced the worst rioting in the history of the city. On a hot afternoon, a white police officer had pulled over a black man for driving drunk in a black neighborhood known as Watts. The driver was, in fact, drunk, and did not resist arrest. However, when the driver's brother and mother arrived so that they could drive the vehicle away, the police officer said no. Instead, the officer called for the vehicle to be impounded. Understandably, the brother and mother were very upset about this unfair treatment, and they began to argue with the officer. Soon, a crowd gathered on the scene. As had happened in Philadelphia a year earlier, blacks in Los Angeles had reached the end of their patience with police brutality.

When the officer placed handcuffs on the brother and mother of the drunk driver, explaining angrily that they were now under arrest for arguing, the crowd exploded in shouting. As more police officers arrived, the crowd started throwing rocks and bottles at the policemen. Then the violence moved through the streets, and cars were turned over and smashed, while businesses were set on fire and looted.

For the six days that rioting continued, smoke from the Watts area could be seen from miles away. In the middle of it all, the Los Angeles police chief, William Parker, made things much worse by referring to those rioting as "monkeys in the zoo." By the time it was all over, 34 people had been killed, 1,032 injured, and 3,952 arrested. Property damage exceeded $40 million.

King was discouraged by the extreme violence in Los Angeles, but he understood why blacks in the North and West were so angry. In the South, King explained, blacks and whites often shared the experience of poverty. So, while blacks had been separated from whites through Jim Crow laws, they did not necessarily live in drastically poorer conditions. Neighborhoods were segregated as a result of unfair laws, not income.

In Northern and Western cities, however, blacks and whites were separated as a result of the poverty many blacks experienced. Because there had never been Jim Crow laws in these areas, many whites simply ignored the conditions blacks lived in, assuming that nothing was wrong and, frankly, often preferring the separation. This kind of segregation was known as "de facto" segregation. It forced blacks to live in horrible ghettos while, just across the city, whites lived in sparkling high-rise buildings and comfortably ignored the poverty only minutes from their doorsteps. As the civil rights movement gained momentum, many blacks in the North and West became more and more frustrated with being ignored in this way.

"When people are voiceless," King would write, "they will have temper tantrums like a little child who has not been paid attention to. And riots are massive temper tantrums from a neglected and voiceless people."

King flew to Los Angeles to speak to the blacks there about how much more effective nonviolence could be. But many blacks in Los Angeles saw King as just an out-of-touch minister from the South who was sticking his nose into something he didn't understand.

"Get out of here, Dr. King! We don't want you!" a man yelled when King spoke to a crowd in Watts.

"Parker's the one who should be here, not you," shouted another man, referring to the Los Angeles police chief. "He should see how we have to live!"

King decided to speak to Parker and present a number of ways that the city could help those who lived in the ghettos. Parker, however, paid little attention to King and rejected all his ideas. King would later write that Chief of Police Parker was as racist as any police chief he had met in the South.

King returned to Atlanta downhearted. He wondered if the civil rights movement had let down blacks in the North and West. Had the very movement that was supposed to have helped them, ignored them? As the summer came to an end, King watched the news of terrible rioting in Chicago and New York, and he decided that it was time for him to do something very different.

King recalled how Gandhi had shown his dedication to the freedom movement in India by living among the poor people. He had cast away all of his money and material possessions in order to point out how wrong it was to separate people based on wealth. Gandhi was the most famous and best-loved leader in all of India, yet he lived the simplest of existences, weaving his own clothes and raising goats for milk and meat.

Finally, King made up his mind.

"You can't really get close to the poor without living and being there with them," King said to reporters as he left Atlanta with his family.

It was the dead of winter, 1966, and the Kings were on their way to Chicago to live in a ghetto.

CHAPTER 12

"Our apartment was on the third floor of a dingy building," Coretta Scott King would later write about their temporary home in Chicago. "As we walked in the hallway of the building, I realized that the floor was not concrete, but bare dirt. The smell of urine was overpowering. We were told that this was because . . . drunks came in from off the street to use the hallway as a toilet."

For their filthy, freezing apartment, the Kings paid $90 a month. In 1966, that was quite a lot. What's more, white tenants on the other side of town paid $80 a month or less for much nicer apartments. King saw that blacks were being taken advantage of, and this was one of the main problems he worked to solve during his time in Chicago.

King named this new movement the

"Chicago Freedom Movement." He hoped to be able to free blacks from the unfair practices of white landlords and real estate brokers. There were more than a million black people in Chicago, but very few of them lived in the better apartments or homes, even though many could have afforded them. Every time blacks tried to rent apartments or buy homes in white neighborhoods, landlords or agents would find some reason to deny them. Making matters worse, the Chicago politicians approved of this form of discrimination and helped create picky regulations that would ensure that blacks and whites remained separate.

After a year of hard work in Chicago, King was frustrated. Although blacks attended rallies and supported the idea of fair housing, they seemed reluctant to work with King. They had more faith in their white mayor, Richard Daley, than in King. After all, Daley had been born and raised in Chicago. How could a minister from Georgia know what blacks in Chicago needed? Daley told King that he had his own plan for dealing with poverty and housing in Chicago, but King saw right away that Daley's plan would not really help blacks.

Worst of all, King discovered that white people in Chicago were violently opposed to having blacks in their neighborhoods. During marches, whites gathered to throw rocks, bottles, and firecrackers at the black demonstrators. King was struck in the head once, falling to the ground before aides rushed to help him. Even Chicago's liberal whites who supported fair housing told King that his demonstrations were only making people angry. Meanwhile, rioting continued in Chicago, much of it right in the Kings' neighborhood. After one particularly long night of gunshots, screaming, and sirens, Coretta decided to return to Atlanta with the children.

Within a month, King would follow his family back home. Before King left, Mayor Daley halfheartedly signed a fair-housing agreement that King had presented to him. But the mayor, whom black people trusted more than they trusted King, filed the agreement away and never made any changes.

The summer of 1967 saw some of the worst rioting in the history of the United States. In Newark, New Jersey, police arrested and beat a black cab driver unconscious for the "crime" of tailgating their car. News of this police brutality spread, and blacks erupted with rioting that left 26 people dead and 725 injured. Less than a week later, rioting broke out in Detroit when police raided a bar in a black neighborhood.

After a week of violence, 43 people had been killed, 1,189 injured, and over 7,000 arrested.

The death and destruction brought about by rioting created what one newspaper reporter called a "fatal death blow to the civil rights movement." Although many white people had been supportive of the work blacks had been doing to gain equal rights, this violence both angered and frightened them. It caused them to turn their backs on the whole movement. Some whites who had supported racially-mixed neighborhoods now began to change their minds.

King refused to believe that the civil rights movement had died. He spent much of 1967 traveling throughout the United States speaking in support of the original nonviolent protests. Rioting had not only stopped the progress of the movement; it had, in fact, caused the movement to lose ground.

"Even if every Negro in the United States comes to think that Negroes ought to riot," King said, "I'm going to stand as that lone voice and say, 'It's impractical. . . . we'll never get our own way that way.'"

King could not seem to reach blacks the way he had been able to years earlier. More and more blacks were raising their fists in anger and shouting the newly popular slogan "Black

Power!" The young men and women of the Student Nonviolent Coordinating Committee (SNCC) looked to leaders such as the fierce Stokely Carmichael, who insisted that blacks must seize power and demand change— not march peacefully while allowing white policemen to beat them. Because so many members of SNCC agreed that blacks should use more force, the group eventually changed its name to the Student *National* Coordinating Committee. Nonviolence was now a thing of the past, the students said, something for old people or out-of-touch leaders like King.

Pulling the nation's attention even further away from the civil rights movement was the Vietnam War. Many Americans felt that the United States was fighting in a war that it should not be involved in and that it could never win. Night after night, news programs showed horrific images from Vietnam, and every day more American soldiers were killed. For many Americans, the energy that had gone into marching for civil rights now went into marching for peace.

There was, perhaps, no one more outspoken about the Vietnam War than Martin Luther King, Jr. King was particularly angry that black soldiers were fighting and dying in an effort to bring "democracy" to a foreign country when they still had so little democracy in their own country.

"The American involvement in Vietnam is nothing less than madness," King announced in a speech in New York City. "Somehow, this madness must cease."

Although King had always been against war and violence, he was suddenly criticized for speaking out publicly against the Vietnam War. Some felt he was joining this popular cause in order to draw attention back to himself. Others felt he should just stick to the civil rights movement. Even President Johnson was angry with King. Johnson was determined to win in Vietnam, and he felt that King, for whom he had done so much, should keep his opinions to himself.

Finally, King decided to regroup and refocus. He understood that much of the anger seething from black people resulted from the frustration of being poor. It was a vicious circle. Many blacks were too poor to get better education. Lack of education meant low-paying jobs. Low-paying jobs meant raising children who often would not receive advantages or a good education. And the cycle would begin all over again.

Because blacks had been treated as second-class citizens for so long, many of them felt a certain sense of shame and worthlessness. King knew that this created anger, too.

"We must say to ourselves and the world," King said to black people in poor areas, "'I am somebody. I am a person. I am a man with dignity and honor.' Tell your children that black people are very beautiful."

In late 1967, King announced the formation of a Poor People's Campaign. Wherever poor people, black or white, were being treated unfairly, King and the Southern Christian Leadership Conference vowed to come to their assistance. King and his aides began making plans for another big march on Washington to take place in the summer of 1968. This time, marchers would camp out in tents right on the Washington Mall until the federal government gave them what they wanted: a $30 billion anti-poverty program. This was a big event that would take a lot of planning.

In the meantime, King focused on helping people who were being mistreated or underpaid in the workplace. That is what took Martin Luther King, Jr., to Memphis, Tennessee, in the spring of 1968.

"Did you get your flowers?" Martin asked

Coretta from a pay phone in the airport as he waited for his flight to Memphis.

Coretta smiled and touched the carnations. They looked real, even though they weren't.

"They're beautiful," Coretta answered. "And they're artificial." Coretta was surprised that Martin had given her artificial flowers, something he had never done before.

"Yes," Martin said. "I wanted to give you something you could always keep."

Later, looking back on that moment, Coretta would write, "They were the last flowers I ever got from Martin. Somehow, in some strange way, he seemed to know how long they would have to last."

When King reached Memphis, the tension in the air was strong. Black sanitation workers had gone on strike to protest both their working conditions and the fact that white workers doing the same job received much higher pay. For a number of days, sanitation workers marched through downtown Memphis to City Hall. Every protestor wore a bold sign that said I AM A MAN. Those on strike wanted to make clear that being treated fairly had less to do with equal pay than with equal status as a human being.

However, the city had no interest in being fair. The mayor completely ignored the sanitation workers' demands. After strikers had walked to City Hall a few times, city officials authorized police to use tear gas and clubs to break up the marches. The strike organizers finally called King, hoping that his presence would change things.

King's enthusiasm and encouragement fired up the strikers. After a particularly rousing speech, it was decided that King would lead a peaceful march on March 22. King called home and excitedly told Coretta that he felt the old spirit of the nonviolent civil rights movement in Memphis. Perhaps this would be the turning point that would put the movement back on the right track.

When a man with a strange accent called a Memphis radio station to say that King would be shot and killed if he marched on the 22nd, King's spirits weren't dampened. He'd been threatened dozens of times before. Even when a rare Tennessee snowstorm dumped a foot of snow in Memphis on the 21st and the march had to be canceled, King remained positive. The march was simply rescheduled for a week later.

On March 28, the streets of downtown Memphis were packed with 6,000 protestors. From the very start, King sensed that something was wrong. The crowd seemed nervous and jittery. King and Abernathy, both leading the march, kept getting shoved from behind.

Suddenly there was shouting and the crash of shattering glass just to the King's left. A group of about sixty black teens and young men who called themselves "the Invaders" had decided to turn the march into a riot.

King and Abernathy ducked and ran to safety, but not before seeing the BLACK POWER signs the Invaders carried as they threw rocks at store windows. The Memphis police reacted immediately with tear gas and beatings. Within minutes, the entire downtown had exploded into terrible violence. When the crowd became too much for the police to handle, officers pulled out rifles and began shooting. Before it all ended, sixty-two people had been badly injured, and one sixteen-year-old boy had been killed.

King Leads March that Turns Violent
Teen Killed in Protest Organized by King
Martin Luther King, Jr., Involved in Riot

King read the headlines of several newspapers the next day and was as depressed as he had ever been about the direction of the civil rights movement. Later that morning, nearly in tears, he called Coretta.

"You're not responsible for it," Coretta told him. "All of the other demonstrations you have organized and led have not turned out this way."

"I was leading it," King responded sadly, "so I will be blamed."

However, within twenty-four hours, King's attitude changed. At a press conference, he talked confidently and firmly about how he would *not* give up, how Memphis would *not* give up, how the civil rights movement would most definitely *not* give up. Another march was planned for April 5. This time, King assured the press, there would be no violence.

"Dr. King, what has happened to you since last night?" one reporter asked, surprised at King's changed outlook. "Have you talked with someone?"

"No, I haven't talked with anyone," King said quietly. "I have only talked with God."

On the evening of April 3, King told Abernathy that he was too tired to address the 2,000 protestors who had gathered at Mason Temple. Perhaps, he suggested, Abernathy could speak instead. But both Abernathy and Jesse Jackson, who had become one of King's closest aides, pleaded with him to encourage his followers. They wanted and needed to hear from *him*. Wearily, King agreed to speak.

That night as King spoke, he mentioned many of the highlights of his involvement in civil rights. He spoke of Birmingham, Selma, the civil rights bill, and even of the little girl who had been so glad he hadn't sneezed when he was stabbed. Finally, he gazed out across the crowd with a faraway look in his eyes.

"Well, I don't know what will happen now," King said. "Like anybody, I would like to live a long life. . . . But I'm not concerned about that now. I just want to do God's will. And He's allowed me to go up to the mountain. And I've looked over. And I've seen the promised land."

A breathless hush seemed to settle over the crowd as King continued.

"I may not get there with you. But I want you to know tonight that we, as a people, will get to the promised land."

It would be King's final speech. That night, as a warm rain tapped on the roof of the Lorraine Motel where King was staying, an escaped convict named James Earl Ray checked into another hotel. From Ray's window, there was a clear view of room 306 at the Lorraine Motel. Ray knew King was staying in that room.

April 4 was a long day of work, planning, and preparation for the next day's march. Finally, in the late afternoon, King returned to his motel. He was in a joyous mood; it looked as though the march would be a success. Just before leaving for dinner, King stood on the balcony outside his room joking with Abernathy and Jackson.

In that lighthearted moment of a spring evening, James Earl Ray stood at the window of his hotel room, peering through the sight of a high-powered rifle. He was aiming at King's head.

Crack!

Instantly, King fell to floor of the balcony, clutching his throat.

"Take cover!" King's aides shouted as Abernathy kneeled beside his friend. For just a moment, King's and Abernathy's eyes met. Abernathy later recalled that King looked terrified.

"It's all right. You'll be okay, Martin," Abernathy whispered desperately as he pressed towels around King's head, trying to stop the growing puddle of blood.

Then King's eyes closed. He would not regain consciousness. At 7:05 p.m. on April 4, 1968, Martin Luther King, Jr., was pronounced dead.

He was only thirty-nine years old.

EPILOGUE:
FAREWELL TO KING

"Now Martin is gone from us. Now we are alone."

These were Ralph Abernathy's first words to the circle of aides and friends who were gathered outside the hospital room where King died. King had often told Abernathy that he should be prepared to take over as leader of the civil rights movement. But Abernathy knew that no one would ever replace King. The entire world knew it.

In Atlanta, Coretta received the news. As shattered as she was by it, she knew she had to remain calm for the sake of her four children. She sat down and did her best to explain what had happened.

"Mommy, should I hate the man who killed my daddy?" Yolanda asked.

"No, darling, your daddy wouldn't want you to do that," Coretta replied, putting her arms around her oldest child.

It was terribly difficult for the children to understand. Surely, it was nearly impossible for Dexter, who was only seven years old, to understand. When Coretta came to his room to tuck him into bed, he looked at his mother in confusion and asked, "But, Mommy, when is Daddy coming *home*?"

Pain and anger are often impossible to separate. So as the country learned about King's assassination, many blacks reacted with rage. It was an unfortunate response to the death of a man who had spent his life preaching peace. Still, riots flared in more than 100 cities in the days following the shooting. Businesses were destroyed, cars burned, thousands were injured, and forty-six people died.

Ironically, one of the few cities where there was no rioting was Memphis. Ralph Abernathy, Coretta, and the three oldest King children flew to Memphis to lead the march that King had planned to lead. It was their way of showing the world that nonviolence was not a thing of the past. In the very city where King had been murdered, 19,000 people marched peacefully and respectfully. There was not one incident of anger or fighting.

Days later, in Atlanta, King's funeral was held. Ebenezer Baptist Church was packed, and an additional 60,000 mourners stood outside the church to listen to the service over loudspeakers. A tape was played of one of the last sermons King had delivered at Ebenezer. In that sermon, he had talked about what he would want said at his own funeral someday: "I'd like somebody to mention that day that . . . Martin Luther King, Jr., tried to give his life serving others. I'd like for somebody to say that day that . . . Martin Luther King, Jr., tried to love somebody. . . . I won't have any money to leave behind. . . . But I just want to leave a committed life behind. Then my living will not be in vain."

In honor of the Poor People's Campaign, King's casket was loaded onto a simple farm wagon and pulled through the streets of Atlanta by two mules. More than 50,000 people marched silently behind the wagon, many of them dressed in overalls to symbolize King's dream of helping poor people—a dream he would now be unable to fulfill. Along the procession route, thousands more stood quietly, some holding signs that read HONOR KING: END RACISM!

Finally, the long, sad procession reached South View Cemetery, where King's grandmother was buried. King was buried near her. And on his tomb were etched the words from one of King's favorite old spirituals—the same words that had ended his famous "I Have a Dream" speech:

> **Free at last, Free at last,**
> **Thank God Almighty**
> **I'm free at last.**

Two months after King's funeral, his accused assassin, James Earl Ray, was captured in London, England. Ray, a high school dropout and a lifelong criminal, admitted to staying in the hotel across from King. He also confessed to owning a rifle like the one that was used in the murder. And though he pleaded guilty and was sentenced to life in prison, Ray later denied shooting King. He claimed that King's murder had been plotted out by a group of people, and that he had played only a minor part.

Most people ignored Ray's comments. After all, his fingerprints had been found on the rifle and the binoculars left behind. But others believed him—including members of the King family. As an adult, Dexter King spoke with Ray and was convinced that Ray was not his father's killer. However, before the mystery could be solved, James Earl Ray died in prison.

Only days after King's assassination, a congressman from Michigan, John Conyers, presented the idea of a national holiday honoring Dr. King. Like everything that King had worked for during his life, acceptance of a Martin Luther King, Jr. Day would take a while—nearly twenty years, in fact. Many lawmakers argued that another national holiday would be too expensive for employers. Some pointed out that there were no other holidays for private citizens; King had not been a President or government official. Still others, like Senator Jesse Helms from North Carolina, felt that King had not been important enough to be honored with a holiday.

Coretta Scott King had been her husband's biggest supporter during his life, and that continued once he was gone. She worked tirelessly to make certain that King's memory and achievements did not fade. In 1968 she established The King Center, which would eventually include a memorial, museum, library, and National Historic Site dedicated to the life and teachings of Dr. King. In 1969, Coretta's *My Life with Martin Luther King, Jr.* was published.

"I have written this book in order to inspire young people to take up my husband's challenge," Coretta explained at the beginning of the book.

In addition, Coretta Scott King never gave up working toward a Martin Luther King, Jr. Day. In 1980, as president of the King Center, Coretta revived the push for a holiday honoring her late husband. She wrote to leaders and politicians all over the United States. An office was set up in Washington, D.C., so that supporters of the holiday could keep the pressure on lawmakers. That same year, Stevie Wonder, a popular singer and songwriter, even wrote a song titled "Happy Birthday": *I just never understood / How a man who died for good / Could not have a day that would / Be set aside for his recognition.*

Finally, President Ronald Reagan signed the holiday bill into law on November 3, 1983. However, the first official Martin Luther King, Jr. Day would not be celebrated until 1986.

The civil rights movement did not suddenly die when King died. It did, however, begin to fade. Ralph Abernathy took over as leader of the SCLC, and many of King's aides, such as Andrew Young and Jesse Jackson, tried to continue with King's plans for the Poor People's Campaign. But things were not the same without King.

Thanks to King's sacrifice and hard work, new laws made unfair treatment of black people illegal. However, racial prejudice and hate crimes continued. Perhaps the discrimination was not as obvious as it had been in the days of Jim Crow laws, but it was often just as destructive.

African Americans were angered and saddened by King's death and by this discrimination in spite of new laws. Some viewed the shooting of King as the final blow and, as a result, turned to the one thing that King had spent his entire adult life preaching against: violence.

Not long before King was killed, he had written, "And I guess one of the great agonies of life is that we are constantly trying to finish that which is unfinishable."

In his wisdom, King had been well aware that "finishing" racism and violence in his lifetime would be impossible. Perhaps it would *never* be possible. Still, King had faith in the goodness of human beings and in a better future—someday. Many times he had repeated, "The arc of history is long, but it bends toward justice." In his lifetime, King had witnessed—and had inspired—the bending of that arc.

Certainly, King had hoped that his legacy would be, at the very least, the seeds of understanding that hate and violence can never bring about good change.

"I am concerned about a better world," King had said. "Through violence you may murder a liar, but you can't establish truth. Through violence you may murder a hater, but you can't murder hate. Darkness cannot put out darkness. Only light can do that."